SIEGFRIED SASSOON'S LONG JOURNEY

A GINIGER BOOK

published in association with

OXFORD UNIVERSITY PRESS

New York   Toronto

1983

SIEGFRIED SASSOON'S LONG JOURNEY

Selections from the Sherston Memoirs

Edited by

PAUL FUSSELL

LIBRARY OF CONGRESS CATALOGING IN PUBLICATION DATA
Sassoon, Siegfried, 1886-1967.
  Siegfried Sassoon's long journey.
  1. World War, 1914-1918—Fiction. I. Fussell,
Paul, 1924- . II. Sassoon, Siegfried, 1886-
1967. The memoirs of George Sherston. 1983.   III. Title.
PR6037.A86M42   1983   823'.912   83-8130
ISBN 0-19-503309-4

Printing (last digit): 9 8 7 6 5 4 3 2 1

Printed in the United States of America

ACKNOWLEDGMENTS

I am grateful to the following for various kinds of help: Theodore Bogacz, Leo Cooper, Stuart Cooper, Patricia Evans, Kenneth Giniger, Anthony Powell, Richard Quaintance, George Sassoon, Roderick Suddaby, Eileen Tweedy, and Michael Willis. I owe a special debt to Gertrude Buckman, who with patience and enterprise located most of the peacetime illustrations in this book. And as always I am grateful to the learned and devoted staff of the Imperial War Museum, who have helped me f nd most of the wartime pictures.

P.F.

Again the dead, the dead again demanding
To be, O now to be remembered strongly—

.   .   .

How can you be believed in, how made certain,
How sought beyond the silences of learning?
And how, revisitants by life envisioned,
Can what we are empower your quiet returning?

Siegfried Sassoon,
from "Words for the Wordless"

INTRODUCTION

The First World War, which lasted more than four years and killed seventeen million people, scored across twentieth-century history a deep dividing line, ugly as the scar of its own trenches. Before the war, the world could seem safely stabilized by monarchies, religious certainties, and patriotic pieties. But afterwards, the world appears recognizably "modern," its institutions precarious, its faith feeble, its choices risky, its very landscapes perverted into the Waste Land. No one contemplating the events of 1914-1918 in relation to the years preceding can quite escape this sense of experience divided into "before" and "after." Thus J. B. Priestley comparing the First War with the Second: "I think the First War cut deeper and played more tricks with time because it was first. . . . If you were born in 1894, as I was, you suddenly saw a great jagged crack in the looking-glass. After that your mind could not escape from the idea of a world that ended in 1914 and another one that began about 1919, with a wilderness of smoke and fury, outside sensible time, lying between them." One reason we understand so readily this scheme of before and after is that we have been taught it by the young writers who found in the First World War their first important literary material and who addressed it with the thrill of discovery that has kept their works fresh and powerful. Writing within their various national styles, Henri Barbusse in France, Erich Maria Remarque in Germany, and Hemingway in America earned their earliest reputations by exploiting this theme of before and after. In England, Edmund Blunden, Robert Graves, and Siegfried Sassoon did the same. All would agree with the Priestley who says, "I left one world to spend an exile in limbo, came out of it to find myself in another world."

Why does Siegfried Sassoon seem so quintessentially English? One reason, surely, is his almost erotic fondness for the pastoral countryside. Another is his devotion to horses and horse culture. Another is his being equally skilled in prose and verse while declining to raise a clamor in either. And finally, there is his preference for experience over abstract thought, or, to put it more bluntly, his lack of interest in ideas. "My brain," he says, "absorbs facts singly, and the process of relating them to one another has always been difficult." When a reviewer observed of his book of poems Counter-Attack (1918) that Sassoon seemed "entirely devoid of intellectual edge," he commented: "But I could have told him that myself." What interests Sassoon instead is appearances, the look of things, especially the look of things in a past affectionately remembered, or even ambiguously remembered: "Oh yes, I see it all, from A to Z!" he says of the front line, recalling it with mingled love and horror at the end of these memoirs. This book is designed to emphasize Sassoon's distinction as an observer and evoker of visible objects, both in peace and war. If the war came close to exterminating Sassoon, it also educated him, teaching him, he writes, "one useful lesson—that on the whole it was very nice to be alive at all." It also developed in him "the habit of observing things with more receptiveness and accuracy than I had ever attempted to do in my undisciplined past."

The countryside he liked to feel alive in was the Weald of Kent, the wooded and agricultural part of that county southeast of London. He was born there in 1886, one of three brothers. His brother Hamo was to be killed at Gallipoli in 1915. The house of his well-to-do family stood at the edge of the green in the village of Matfield (here, in these fictionalized memoirs, "Butley"), a few miles from Tunbridge Wells. When Siegfried was five, his Spanish-Jewish father left his wife and died soon after. The boy grew up protected and encouraged by his mother, who had artistic and literary relatives. She knew critics and editors like Edmund Gosse and Edward Marsh, who interested themselves both in the boy and in his early verses. (The "Aunt Evelyn" of these memoirs is a fiction.) He went to Marlborough College (here, "Ballboro"), whose headmaster told him as he left, "Try to be more sensible." He proceeded to Clare College, Cambridge, where he began reading law but shifted to history and finally to nothing at all, leaving after four terms and returning to Kent. Delighted to be reinstalled at home, far from demands that he think, he collected books, read (with heavy emphasis on the hunting whimsies of R. S. Surtees), played cricket and golf, fox-hunted, and mooned shyly about, versifying in the vague sentimental mode customary in pre-war minor poetry. Between the ages of nineteen and twenty-six he published privately nine volumes of dreamy romantic verse, a fact he omits entirely from the "outdoor" version of his life he presents here.

This idyll was ended by the outbreak of war on August 4, 1914. He was healthy, naïve, unthinkingly patriotic, and horsy, and by August 5 he was in the uniform of a cavalry trooper. He was twenty-eight years old. Soon he transferred to the infantry and became a second lieutenant in the Royal Welch Fusiliers. Before long he was in action in France, where his

x

initial enthusiasm gradually yielded to outrage as he learned that the war was not at all the heroic, high-minded operation pictured by propaganda. He was a brave and able officer, and his men, with many of whom he was in love, liked him for his kindness to them. One remembers: "It was only once in a blue moon that we had an officer like Mr. Sassoon." He turned fierce after his friend, fellow-officer David Thomas ("Dick Tiltwood"), was killed. Lieutenant D. C. Thomas had been Sassoon's current ideal companion, a Galahad figure,

> One whose yellow head was kissed
> By the gods, who thought about him
> Till they couldn't do without him.

("There is no doubt that I am still a Pre-Raphaelite," Sassoon once wrote in his diary.)

Conceiving that the cause of David's death was the Germans rather than the war, Sassoon set himself to avenge him by bolder and bolder forays against the enemy. These helped earn him the nickname "Mad Jack" from his platoon. He won the Military Cross for bringing in wounded under fire, and he was soon wounded in the shoulder himself. While convalescing at home, pity for his men grew on him, together with a conviction that the war was a fraud, a swindle practiced on the troops by bellicose civilians at home and their viceregents, the staff, safely ensconced back at the Base. He began writing anti-homefront poems satirizing the cruelty and complacency of those whose relation to the war was rather forensic than empirical. These poems were very different from the ones he'd written before the war. Then, he had been content to turn out courteous little verses like this:

NIMROD IN SEPTEMBER

> When half the drowsy world's abed
> And misty morning rises red,
> With jollity of horn and lusty cheer,
> Young Nimrod urges on his dwindling rout;
> Along the yellowing coverts we can hear
> His horse's hoofs thud hither and about:
> In mulberry coat he rides and makes
> Huge clamour in the sultry brakes.

Before the war his poems had celebrated Dryads, "roundelays and jocund airs," dulcimers and shoon, daffodillies, shepherds, and "ye patient kine," Indeed, as the eminent pastoralist Edmund Blunden once said, "No poet of twentieth-century England . . . was originally more romantic and floral than young Siegfried Sassoon from Kent." But now he unleashed a talent *for irony and satire and contumely that had been sleeping all during his pastoral youth:*

"THEY"

The Bishop tells us: "When the boys come back
They will not be the same; for they'll have fought
In a just cause: they lead the last attack
On Anti-Christ; their comrades' blood has bought
New right to breed an honourable race,
They have challenged Death and dared him face to face."

"We're none of us the same!" the boys reply.
"For George lost both his legs; and Bill's stone blind;
Poor Jim's shot through the lungs and like to die;
And Bert's gone syphilitic: you'll not find
A chap who's served that hasn't found some change."
And the Bishop said: "The ways of God are strange!"

(As Wilfred Owen noticed, "Sassoon admires Thos. Hardy more than anybody living.")

In the blank verse in which formerly he had described rural delights he now delivered outdoor views of a different sort:

We'd gained our first objective hours before
While dawn broke like a face with blinking eyes,
Pallid, unshaved and thirsty, blind with smoke.
Things seemed all right at first. We held their line,
With bombers posted, Lewis guns well placed,
And clink of shovels deepening the shallow trench.
   The place was rotten with dead; green clumsy legs
High-booted, sprawled and grovelled along the saps
And trunks, face downward, in the sucking mud,
Wallowed like trodden sand-bags loosely filled;
And naked sodden buttocks, mats of hair,
Bulged, clotted heads slept in the plastering slime.
And then the rain began—the jolly old rain!

Back home the recruiting posters depicted women proudly watching the troops march away ("Women of Britain Say—'GO!' "), and Phyllis Dare's music-hall song was heard everywhere:

Oh, we don't want to lose you,
But we think you ought to go;

For your King and your Country
Both need you so.

We shall want you and miss you,
But with all our might and main
We will thank you, cheer you, kiss you,
When you come back again.

Sassoon's response:

GLORY OF WOMEN

You love us when we're heroes, home on leave,
Or wounded in a mentionable place.
You worship decorations; you believe
That chivalry redeems the war's disgrace.
You make us shells. You listen with delight,
By tales of dirt and danger fondly thrilled.
You crown our distant ardours while we fight,
And mourn our laurelled memories when we're killed.
You can't believe that British troops "retire"
When hell's last horror breaks them, and they run,
Trampling the terrible corpses—blind with blood.
   O German mother dreaming by the fire,
   While you are knitting socks to send your son
   His face is trodden deeper in the mud.

Popular as poems like these were with the young avant-garde back in London, they scandalized the respectable. The critic John Middleton Murry found Sassoon's performances "verses, . . . not poetry," mere "violent journalism": "He has no calm," Murry wrote, "therefore he conveys no terror; he has no harmony, therefore he cannot pierce us with the anguish of discord." Indeed, "Mr. Sassoon's mind is a chaos." Not certain whether to back this horse or not, Gosse straddled the critical fence, saying of Sassoon's The Old Huntsman and Other Poems (1917): "His temper is not altogether to be applauded, for such sentiments must tend to relax the effort of the struggle, yet they can hardly be reproved when conducted with so much honesty and courage. . . ." One might imagine that the scandal produced by Sassoon's anti-war poems would have been noticed everywhere in lettered England. But two years after the Armistice Rider Haggard confesses that he's never heard of Siegfried Sassoon and wonders whether he's not just another "Jew of the advanced school," like Bakst, Epstein, or Proust. Urged by an acquaintance to read Sassoon's poems, he finally does so, to find them "feeble and depressing rubbish."

But Sassoon was maturing an outrage more offensive than a few poems calling into question the official, sanitized view of the war. In July 1917, encouraged by H. W. Massingham ("Markington"), editor of the liberal weekly the Nation, and Bertrand Russell ("Thornton Tyrell"), he set off his own bombshell. He published his famous document "A Soldier's Declaration," in which he explained "his grounds for refusing to serve further in the army":

I am making this statement as an act of wilful defiance of military authority, because I believe that the war is being deliberately prolonged by those who have the power to end it.

I am a soldier, convinced that I am acting on behalf of soldiers. I believe that this war, upon which I entered as a war of defence and liberation, has now become a war of aggression and conquest. I believe that the purposes for which I and my fellow-soldiers entered upon this war should have been so clearly stated as to have made it impossible to change them, and that, had this been done, the objects which actuated us would now be attainable by negotiation.

I have seen and endured the sufferings of the troops, and I can no longer be a party to prolong these sufferings for ends which I believe to be evil and unjust.

I am not protesting against the conduct of the war, but against the political errors and insincerities for which the fighting men are being sacrificed.

On behalf of those who are suffering now I make this protest against the deception which is being practiced on them; also I believe that I may help to destroy the callous complacence with which the majority of those at home regard the continuance of agonies which they do not share, and which they have not sufficient imagination to realize.

S. Sassoon.

He expected to be court-martialed for this, the attendant publicity, he hoped, adding force to the tiny public sentiment in favor of ending the war through a negotiated peace. Instead, assisted by his friend and fellow Royal Welch Fusilier Robert Graves ("David Cromlech"), he was sent by the authorities before a medical board, as if anyone voicing such pacific sentiments must be deranged. The medical officers found him overstrained and consigned him to a comfortable army mental hospital, Craiglockhart (here, "Slateford"), near Edinburgh.

In the hospital he met a poetical fan of his, Lieutenant Wilfred Owen, currently being treated for combat neurasthenia. Owen's enthusiasm for Sassoon's poetry and person was unbounded. He wrote his mother: "I have just been reading *Siegfried Sassoon, and am feeling at a very high pitch of emotion. Nothing like his trench life sketches has ever been written or ever will be written.*" Owen quickly sought out his idol and sent this report to a friend: "*He is very tall and stately, with a fine firm chisel'd (how's that?) head, ordinary short brown hair. The general expression of his face is one of boredom. . . . The last thing he said was 'Sweat your guts out writing poetry.' 'Eh?' says I. 'Sweat your guts out, I say!' He also warned me against early publishing. . . . He himself is thirty! Looks under 25!*" (Typically, in the horsy *Memoirs of George Sherston* Sassoon says nothing about this meeting, while dealing with it extensively in his report on his literary life, *Siegfried's Journey*.)

In the hospital, guilt at the ease and safety he had purchased by his gesture of disobedience began to trouble him, and he finally persuaded his psychiatrist to let him go back to the war. His psychiatrist was Dr. W. H. R. Rivers (1864-1922), the well-known Cambridge physiologist and anthropologist, a bachelor 53-year-old Royal Army Medical Corps captain when Sassoon encountered him. In one sense Rivers is the real hero of "George Sherston's" memoirs, and the only person whose name Sassoon has not changed. His memory was a lifelong presence for Sassoon, who much later, in 1952, wrote in his diary: "*I should like to meet Rivers in 'the next world.' It is difficult to believe that such a man as he could be extinguished.*" Sped on his way by Rivers, he returned to active service, at first in Egypt and Palestine. But he was transferred back to the Western Front after the German attack of March 1918, and in July he was wounded again, this time in the head, and sent home for good.

After the war he found himself caught up in London literary life, especially that branch of it espousing a genteel socialism, and for a time he worked as literary editor of the socialist *Daily Herald*. But when he was alone he was trembly and tired, afflicted by nightmares of the war. He felt a vague impulse to write something more sustained than lyric poems but wasn't certain what it should be. A long poem? A play? Or did he have a talent for prose? For fiction? For memoir? Later, he remembered talking with Gosse shortly after the Armistice:

> During our talk he strongly urged me to undertake a long poem which would serve as a peg on which—for the general public— my reputation would hang. He suggested that I might draw on my sporting experiences for typical country figures—the squire, the doctor, the parson, and so on. He was, of course, partly influenced by anxiety that I should divert my mind from the war. At the time I thought the idea unworthy of serious consideration.

Too much, perhaps, like a replay of George Crabbe's The Parish Register and The Borough. But Gosse's suggestion, if mistaken in its particulars, proved fruitful as Sassoon continued to meditate what he should write. As he tells his diary late one night in March 1921:

> I walked back from the Reform [Club] under a black but starful sky, feeling dangerously confident in myself and the masterpiece that I'll be writing five, ten, fifteen, or twenty years hence. That masterpiece has become a perfectly definite object in my existence, but it is curious, and rather disquieting, that I always dream of it as a novel or a prose drama, rather than as a poem or series of poems. . . . The theme of my "masterpiece" demands great art and great qualities of another kind.

It's clear that he's thinking of writing a book registering subtly and in the process justifying his homosexuality. His masterpiece, he says,

> is to be one of the stepping-stones across the raging (or lethargic) river of intolerance which divides creatures of my temperament from a free and unsecretive existence among their fellow-men. . . . O, that unwritten book! Its difficulties are overwhelming.

Eighteen months later he's still obsessed with this urgent but cloudy project. "My whole life has become involved," he says, "in an internal resolve to prepare my mind for a big effort of creation. I want to write a book called The Man Who Loved the World, in which I will embody my whole passionate emotionalism toward every experience which collides with my poetic sensitiveness." But alas, "At present I have not any idea of the architectural plan of this edifice."

But finally he got it: he would write a fictionalized autobiography elegizing his young friends killed in the war. "The dead . . . are more real than the living," he wrote in his diary in 1922, "because they are complete." At the same time he would try to understand what the events of 1914-1918 had done to him and his pre-war world, what their relation was, if any, to that pastoral quietude so rudely displaced. Knowing now what he wanted to do, in 1926 he embarked on twenty years of obsessive prose writing. In six volumes of artful memoirs he revisited the war and lovingly recovered the contrasting scene of gentle self-indulgence and pastoral beauty preceding it. At first uncertain of the value of his work, he sent some manuscript pages to Gosse, who replied: "I think you will be anxious for a word from me, and so I write provisionally to say that I am delighted with it so far. There is no question at all that you must go on steadily. It will be an extraordinarily original book. . . ." But as further pages arrived, Gosse was moved to reprehend a part of Sassoon he's always been uncomfortable with, his impulse to irony and self-distrust: "You are not called upon," he reminded Siegfried, "to draw a sarcastic picture of a slack and idle young man. . . . Remember, no satire and no sneering!"

The first volume, Memoirs of a Fox-Hunting Man, was published in 1928, a moment which brought forth two other classics of innocence savaged by twentieth-century events, Blunden's memoir Undertones of War and, in Germany, Remarque's novel Im Westen Nichts Neues. Two years later, just as Graves was publishing Good-Bye to All That and Hemingway A Farewell to Arms, Sassoon brought out his second volume, Memoirs of an Infantry Officer. And in 1936 Sherston's Progress completed the trilogy he finally titled The Memoirs of George Sherston. It is from that trilogy that the text of this book has been excerpted. Sassoon's narrative, even when cut as it is here, is largely self-explanatory, but now and then I've supplied, in italics, a bit of background or explanation. And I've introduced some of Sassoon's poems at points where they flesh out a theme similar to the one registered in the prose, without meaning to suggest that the poem was necessarily written then.

The story he tells here is that of a shy, awkward, extremely limited young country gentleman acquainted only with hunting and cricket and golf who learns about the greater adult world the hardest way—by perceiving and absorbing the details of its most shocking war. One irony is that Sherston is removed from the aimlessness of his rural life not by, say, a career in the City, which before the war might have been thought the appropriate antidote to idleness; he's removed from it by an alternative quite needlessly excessive, the hell of the trenches. The action of The Memoirs of George Sherston is the transformation of a boy into a man, able at last to transfer his affection for horses first to people, and finally to principles. But this transformation is slow and belated. Sherston is over thirty before he begins to master the facts of life, instructed at one point by seeing "an English soldier lying by the road with a horribly smashed head." Only now is he able to perceive that "life, for the majority of the population, is an unlovely struggle against unfair odds, culminating in a cheap funeral." One reason Sherston learns so slowly is that his character is so inconsistent and unfixed. He is never certain what he is. "He varied," Graves remembers, "between happy warrior and bitter pacifist." And his company second-in-command, Vivian de Sola Pinto ("Velmore"), notes a similar confusion. "It seemed to me a strange paradox," he recalls, "that the author of these poems [in Counter-Attack] full of burning indignation against war's cruelty should also be a first-rate soldier and a most aggressive company commander." It is out of such queer antitheses and ironies that Sassoon constructs these memoirs.

Of course every account of front-line experience in the First World War is necessarily ironic because such experience was so much worse than anyone expected. If in Good-Bye to All That Graves's irony is broad and rowdy, in The Memoirs of George Sherston Sassoon's is quiet and subtle. An example is the way he deals with the theme of horses and warfare, which is to say the way he relates the war part of his memoirs to the earlier pastoral part. In a quiet way, the memoirs become an ironic disclosure of the fate of cavalry—the traditional important military arm in the world before the war—in the new, quite unanticipated war of static confrontation across a pocked, pitted, and impassable No Man's Land. In Sherston's youth the cavalry was virtually the equivalent of the Army. But the machine gun and massed artillery changed all that, and almost all the one million horses used by the British army were put to work ignominiously behind the lines only, hauling rations and ammunitions. And a half-million were killed even then. What happened to the pre-war cavalry tradition for both Allies and Central Powers can be inferred from the production figures for machine guns. In 1915, the British manufactured 1,700. In 1916, 9,600. In 1917, 19,000. The war was inexorably becoming a heavy-duty enterprise, and the swank of cavalry was only one of the colorful things it swept away.

Once this trilogy of memoirs was finished, Sassoon began another set. As if dissatisfied now with the degree of fiction he'd imposed on his experience, he began reviving the past all over again, writing now what he calls his "real auto-biography," this time as "Siegfried Sassoon" rather than "George Sherston." The result was a second trilogy, more true to fact this time, comprising The Old Century and Seven More Years (1938), The Weald of Youth (1942), and Siegfried's Progress (1945). But remote from fact as here and there it may be, the earlier trilogy seems the more persuasive of the two attempts to capture the past. "I am a firm believer in the Memoirs," Sassoon once said.

If Sherston was depicted as an athletic, non-literary youth, in the second trilogy Sassoon reveals himself more accurately as a poet extremely ambitious of success among the artistically powerful of London. "Sherston," he says, "was a simplified version of my 'outdoor self.' He was denied the complex advantage of being a soldier poet." But both characters, representing the two sides of himself he was never sure cohered into a whole, are notable for modesty and understatement, as well as a certain "chuckle-headed inconsistency," as he puts it. But smile as he may with amusement and pity at his former self, Sassoon's lifetime devotion to the young man he once was has something undeniably narcissistic about it, and in this he resembles another cunning twentieth-century memoirist, Christopher Isherwood. Both have created careers by plowing and re-plowing their variously furtive pasts, revealing something different with each rendering. Isherwood's shameful-proud relation to "Christopher" is similar to Siegfried's relation to "George." Thus Sassoon writes in his diary, "What it amounts to is this, that I must behave naturally, keeping one side of my mind aloof, a watchful critic. One part of me . . . is the player on the stage. But I must also be the audience, and not an indulgent one either." It is this very self-conscious awareness of himself as a performer uttering lines that gives much of The Memoirs of George Sherston its special quality, as in the scene in the hospital (pp. 122-23) where he indicates the different things appropriate for him to utter in front of various audiences.

Aesthetes and hearties: that opposition, still a popular jocular way for university students to divide each other up, seemed in Sassoon's day a significant set of polar categories, and it was natural for him to conceive of the range of his own character by means of that formula. The polarities of horseman and artist are nicely indicated by two adjacent diary entries he made in 1920:

Oct 20   Bought mare.
Oct 27   Bought Pickering Aldine poets (53 vols)

and a little later he writes, "Inconsistency—double life—as usual. . . ." What he has done in The Memoirs of George Sherston is to objectify one-half of the creature leading this double life, the half identifiable as the sensitive but mindless athlete, and separate it from the other half, that of the much-cossetted aspirant poet, taken up by Lady Ottoline Morrell, Robert Ross, and other useful figures of the salons. Aestheticism, the actual milieu of his family and friends, vanishes from George Sherston's story. Hence the unsophisticated Aunt Evelyn replaces his actual mother and aunt and uncle, respectively painter, editor, and sculptor. Why does he jettison this Pateresque aspect of himself and his environs? Because, I think, he hopes to show the effect of the war on a more representative and ordinary man, not the man of sensibility and privilege he actually was—rich, literary, musical, arty, careerist. The Memoirs is in part a thirties pacifist document, like Vera Brittain's Testament of Youth (1933); and for it to work it must persuade the reader that the condition of the protagonist is not excessively distant from his own.

During the thirties Sassoon, active in pacifist causes, was distressed to witness Europe moving steadily toward war again. In 1933, at the age of forty-seven, he married and had one son, George. He continued to write poetry, but most critics found this later work feeble compared with his performance as a "war poet." "My renown as a W.P.," he observed, "has now become a positive burden to me." In 1957 he became a Roman Catholic, and in 1967 he died at the age of eighty. But as he seemed to recognize himself, the interesting part of his life was the earlier part, which he revisited repeatedly, recalling twice over in superb prose the Edwardian and Georgian world of his youth and the war that shattered it forever.

A word about the illustrations in this book. Ghastly as some of the front-line photographs are, they are the work of rose-tinted lenses and don't come close to rendering the full actuality. Until 1916 there was little official photography on the Western Front, and when picture-taking was permitted on a large scale the photographer was regarded as a mere employee of the propaganda effort. Consequently the corpses shown tend to be German, not British; the nightmare destruction is largely of enemy works, not one's own. The photographs are designed to convey two main points: that the Huns are wild beasts who deserve to be extirpated; and that despite hardships bravely borne the British are going to win. Pictures are very often posed, and it's clear that the subjects have been adjured not to look downhearted. Still, if we darken the implicit misery by about 30 per cent we'll get an idea of what things looked like to Sassoon and his fellow soldiers. Billions of words have been written about the First World War, most of them deploring the arrangements, leadership, politics, and administration of that event. But "understand" it as we may, we'll never come close to it until we add the feeling inhering in moments when, reading this prose and looking at these pictures, we shake our heads and say to ourselves, "Poor guys. Poor guys."

Historians and literalists should note that the relation of photographs to text here does not pretend to be precise. Because Sassoon has chosen to represent not himself but a credible simulacrum named George Sherston, in presenting the illustrations I have felt free likewise to honor the artistic idea rather than the literal fact. Obviously few of the photographs can depict Sassoon's actual military unit or real geographical circumstances. Readers curious about what they do depict will find that information in the list of captions at the end, although I hope they will not turn there before experiencing the book.

Princeton
July 1983

Paul Fussell

SIEGFRIED SASSOON'S LONG JOURNEY

My CHILDHOOD was a queer and not altogether happy one. Circumstances conspired to make me shy and solitary. My father and mother died before I was capable of remembering them. I was an only child, entrusted to the care of an unmarried aunt who lived quietly in the country. My aunt was no longer young when I began to live in her comfortable, old-fashioned house with its large, untidy garden. She had settled down to her local interests, seldom had anyone to stay with her, and rarely left home. She was fond of her two Persian cats, busied herself sensibly with her garden, and was charitably interested in the old and rheumatic inhabitants of the village. Beyond this, the radius of her activities extended no further than the eight or ten miles which she could cover in a four-wheeled dogcart driven by Tom Dixon, the groom. The rest of the world was what she described as "beyond calling distance."

Dixon was a smart young man who would have preferred a livelier situation. It was he who persuaded my aunt to buy me my first pony. I was then nine years old.

I have said that my childhood was not altogether a happy one. This must have been caused by the absence of companions of my own age. . . . As a consequence of my loneliness I created in my childish day-dreams an ideal companion who became much more of a reality than such unfriendly boys as I encountered at Christmas parties. . . . Among a multitude of blurred memories, my "dream friend" has cropped up with an odd effect of importance which makes me feel that he must be worth a passing mention. The fact is that, as soon as I began to picture in my mind the house and garden where I spent so much of my early life, I caught sight of my small, long-vanished self with this other non-existent boy standing beside him. And, though it sounds silly enough, I feel queerly touched by the recollection of that companionship. For some reason which I cannot explain, the presence of that "other boy" made my childhood unexpectedly clear, and brought me close to a number of things which, I should have thought, would have faded forever. For instance, I have only just remembered the tarnished mirror which used to hang in the sunless passage which led to my schoolroom, and how, when I secretly stared at my small, white face in this mirror, I could hear the sparrows chirping in the ivy which grew thickly outside the windows. Somehow the sight of my own reflection increased my loneliness, till the voice of my aunt speaking to one of the servants on the stairs made me start guiltily away. . . .

And now, as I look up from my writing, these memories also seem like reflections in a glass, reflections which are becoming more and more easy to distinguish. Sitting here, alone with my slowly moving thoughts, I rediscover many little details otherwise dead and forgotten with all who shared that time; and I am inclined to loiter among them as long as possible.

That first pony is clearly visible to me. . . .

When I began my rides on Rob Roy, Dixon used to walk beside me. Our longest expedition led to a place about three miles from home. Down in the Weald were some large hop-farms, and the hop-kilns were interesting objects. It was unusual to find more than two hop-kilns on a farm; but there was one which had twenty, and its company of white cowls was clearly visible from our house on the hill. As a special treat Dixon used to take me down there. Sitting on Rob Roy at the side of the road I would count them over and over again,

and Dixon would agree that it was a wonderful sight. I felt that almost anything might happen in a world which could show me twenty hop-kilns neatly arranged in one field.

I had always been given to understand that I had a delicate constitution. This was one of the reasons which my Aunt urged against my being sent to school when Mr. Pennett, the pink-faced solicitor who had charge of our affairs, paid us one of his periodic visits and the problem of my education was referred to in my presence. The solicitor used to come down from London for the day. In acknowledgment of his masculinity my aunt always conceded him the head of the table at lunch. I can remember him carving a duck with evident relish, and saying in somewhat unctuous tones, "Have you reconsidered, my dear Miss Evelyn, the well-worn subject of a school for our young friend on my left?"

And I can hear my aunt replying in a fluttering voice that she had always been nervous about me since I had pneumonia (though she knew quite well that it was only slight inflammation of the lungs, and more than two years ago at that). Fixing my gaze on his fat pearl tie-pin, I wondered whether I really should ever go to school, and what it would feel like when I got there.

Emboldened by the fact that I was going out hunting with an inward purpose of my own, I clip-clopped alongside of Dixon with my head well in the air. The cold morning had made my fingers numb, but my thoughts moved freely in a warmer climate of their own. I was being magnetized to a distant meet of the hounds, not so much through my sporting instinct as by the appeal which Denis Milden had made to my imagination. That he would be there was the idea uppermost in my mind. My fears lest I should again make a fool of myself were, for the moment, as far below me as my feet. Humdrum home life was behind me; in the freshness of the morning I was setting out for an undiscovered country. . . .

My reverie ended when Sheila slithered on a frozen puddle and Dixon told me to pay attention to what I was doing and not slouch about in the saddle. Having brought me back to reality he inspected his watch and said we were well up to time. A mile or two before we got to the meet he stopped at an inn, where he put our horses into the stable for twenty minutes, "to give them a chance to stale." Then, seeing that I was looking rather pinched with the cold, he took me indoors and ordered a large glass of hot milk, which I should be jolly glad of, he said, before the day was out. The inn-parlour smelt of stale liquor, but I enjoyed my glass of milk.

The meet itself was an intensified rendering of my initiatory one. I was awed by my consciousness of having come twelve miles from home. And the scene was made significant by the phrase "one of their best meets." In the light of that phrase everything appeared a little larger than life; voices seemed louder, coats a more raucous red, and the entire atmosphere more acute with imminent jeopardy than at Finchurst Green. Hard-bitten hunting men rattled up in gigs, peeled off their outer coverings, and came straddling along the crowded lane to look for their nags. Having found them, they spoke in low tones to the groom and swung themselves importantly into the saddle as though there were indeed some desperate business on hand. . . .

Heron's Gate was a featureless wayside inn at the foot of a green knoll. I had not yet caught a glimpse of Denis when the procession moved away toward Park Wood, but I looked upward and identified the bulky black Windmill, which seemed to greet me with a friendly wave of its sails, as much as to say, "Here I am, you see—a lot bigger than they marked me on the map!" The Windmill consoled me; it seemed less inhuman, in its own way, than the brusque and bristling riders around me. When we turned off the road and got on to a sodden tussocked field, they all began to be in a hurry; their horses bucked and snorted and shook their heads as they shot past me—the riders calling out to one another with uncouth matitudinal jocularities.

· · ·

Where we rode the winter sunshine was falling warmly into the wood, though the long grass in the shadows was still flaked with frost. A blackbird went scolding away among the undergrowth, and a jay was setting up a clatter in an ivied oak. Some distance off Jack Pitt was shouting "Yoi-over" and tooting his horn in a leisurely sort of style. Then we turned a corner and came upon Denis. He had pulled his pony across the path, and his face wore a glum look which, as I afterwards learnt to know, merely signified that, for the moment, he had found nothing worth thinking about. The heavy look lifted as I approached him with a faltering smile, but he nodded at me with blunt solemnity, as if what thoughts he had were elsewhere.

"Morning. So you managed to get here." That was all I got by way of greeting. Somewhat discouraged, I could think of no conversational continuance. But Dixon gave him the respectful touch of the hat due to a "proper little sportsman" and, more enterprising than I, supplemented the salute with "Bit slow in finding this morning, sir?"

"Won't be much smell to him when they do. Sun's too bright for that." He had the voice of a boy, but his manner was severely grown-up.

There was a brief silence, and then his whole body seemed to stiffen as he stared fixedly at the undergrowth. Something rustled the

7

dead leaves; not more than ten feet from where we stood, a small russet animal stole out on to the path and stopped for a photographic instant to take a look at us. It was the first time I had ever seen a fox, though I have seen a great many since—both alive and dead. By the time he had slipped out of sight again I had just begun to realize what it was that had looked at me with such human alertness. Why I should have behaved as I did I will not attempt to explain, but when Denis stood up in his stirrups and emitted a shrill "Huick-holler," I felt spontaneously alarmed for the future of the fox.

"Don't do that; they'll catch him!" I exclaimed.

The words were no sooner out of my mouth than I knew I had made another fool of myself. Denis gave me one black look and galloped off to meet the huntsman, who could already be heard horn-blowing in our direction in a maximum outburst of energy.

"Where'd ye see 'im cross, sir?" he exclaimed, grinning at Denis with his great purple face, as he came hustling along with a few of his hounds at his horse's heels.

Denis indicated the exact spot; a moment later the hounds had hit off the line, and for the next ten or fifteen minutes I was so preoccupied with my exertions in following Dixon up and down Park Wood that my indiscretion was temporarily obliterated.

· · ·

Denis, as usual, had detached himself from his immediate surroundings, and was keeping an alert eye on the huntsman's head as
it bobbed up and down along the far side of the fence. Dixon then
made his only reference to my recent misconception of the relation-
ship between foxes and hounds. "Young Mr. Milden won't think
much of you if you talk like that. He must have thought you a regular booby!" Flushed and mortified, I promised to be more careful in
future. But I knew only too well what a mollycoddle I had made myself in the estimation of the proper little sportsman on whom I had
hoped to model myself. . . . "*Don't do that! they'll catch him!*" . . .
It was too awful to dwell on.

I loved the early morning; it was luxurious to lie there, half-
awake, and half-aware that there was a pleasantly eventful day in
front of me. . . . Presently I would get up and lean on the window-
ledge to see what was happening in the world outside. . . . There
was a starling's nest under the window where the jasmine grew thick-
est, and all of a sudden I heard one of the birds dart away with a soft
flurry of wings. Hearing it go, I imagined how it would fly boldly
across the garden; soon I was up and staring at the tree-tops which

9

loomed motionless against a flushed and brightening sky. Slipping into some clothes I opened my door very quietly and tiptoed along the passage and down the stairs. There was no sound except the first chirping of the sparrows in the ivy. I felt as if I had changed since the Easter holidays. The drawing-room door creaked as I went softly in and crept across the beeswaxed parquet floor. Last night's half-consumed candles and the cat's half-empty bowl of milk under the gate-legged table seemed to belong neither here nor there, and my own silent face looked queerly at me out of the mirror. And there was the familiar photograph of "Love and Death," by Watts, with its secret meaning which I could never quite formulate in a thought, though it often touched me with a vague emotion of pathos. When I unlocked the door into the garden the early morning air met me with its cold purity; on the stone step were the bowls of roses and delphiniums and sweet peas which Aunt Evelyn had carried out there before she went to bed; the scarlet disc of the sun had climbed an inch above the hills. Thrushes and blackbirds hopped and pecked busily on the dew-soaked lawn, and a pigeon was cooing monotonously from the belt of woodland which sloped from the garden toward the Weald. Down there in the belt of river-mist a goods train whistled as it puffed steadily away from the station with a distinctly heard clanking of buffers. How little I knew of the enormous world beyond that valley and those low green hills.

Tom Dixon was still about the place to pitchfork me into the village cricket team; and it happened that it was on a showery June morning, when I was setting out for one of the Butley matches, that I received the first really uncomfortable letter from Mr. Pennett. We were playing over at Rotherden, which meant an early start, as it was fourteen miles away. So I slipped the letter into my pocket unopened and perused it at intervals later on in the day. . . . Mr. Pennett . . . had conscientiously dictated to his clerk a couple of pages of expostulation and advice with the unmistakable object of interfering with me as much as possible. . . .

The air was Elysian with early summer and the shadows of steep white clouds were chasing over the orchards and meadows; sunlight

sparkled on green hedgerows that had been drenched by early morning showers. As I was carried past it all I was lazily aware through my dreaming and unobservant eyes that this was the sort of world I wanted. For it was my own countryside, and I loved it with an intimate feeling, though all its associations were crude and incoherent. I cannot think of it now without a sense of heartache, as if it contained something which I have never quite been able to discover.

It was now an accepted fact that I had quitted Cambridge University. During that autumn I was limply incorporating myself with Aunt Evelyn's localized existence. Nothing was being said on the subject of what I was going to do, and I cannot remember that the problem was perplexing my thoughts, or that I felt any hankerings for more eventful departments of human experience. I was content to take it easy until something happened. But since I had no responsibilities and no near relatives except my aunt, whose connection with the world beyond her own "round of calls" was confined to a few old friends who seldom wrote to her, the things which could happen were humdrum and few.

"What are you doing to-day, George?" asks Aunt Evelyn, as she gets up from the breakfast table to go down to the kitchen to interview the cook.

"Oh, I shall probably bike over to Amblehurst after lunch for a round of golf," I reply.

Over at Amblehurst, about four miles away, there is a hazardless nine-hole course round Squire Maundle's sheep-nibbled park. The park faces south-west, sloping to a friendly little river—the Neaze—which at that point, so I have been told, though I have never troubled to verify it—divides the counties of Kent and Sussex. . . . My progress up and down the park from one undersized green to another is accompanied by the temperate clamour of sheep-bells (and in springtime by the loud litanies of baa-ing lambs and anxious ewes).

In my spontaneous memories of Amblehurst . . . the sun is in my eyes as I drive off at the "long hole" down to the river, and I usually slice my ball into a clump of may trees. I am "trying to do a good score"—a purpose which seldom survives the first nine holes—but only half my attention is concentrated on the game. I am wondering, perhaps, whether that parcel from the second-hand bookshop at Reading will have arrived by the afternoon post; or I am vaguely musing about my money affairs; or thinking what a relief it is to have escaped from the tyranny of my Tripos at Cambridge. Outside the park the village children are making a shrill hubbub as they come out of school. But the sun is reddening beyond the straight-rising smoke of the village chimneys, and I must sling my clubs across my shoulder and mount my bicycle to pedal my way along the narrow autumn-smelling lanes. And when I get home Aunt Evelyn will be there to pour out my tea and tell me all about the Jumble Sale this afternoon; it was such a success, they made more than six pounds for the Mission to Deep-sea Fishermen.

I had been taking a walk every afternoon. I usually went five or six miles, but they soon became apathetic ones, and I was conscious of having no genuine connection with the countryside. Other people owned estates, or rented farms, or did something countrified; but I only walked along the roads or took furtive short cuts across the fields of persons who might easily have bawled at me if they had caught

sight of me. And I felt shy and "out of it" among the local land-owners—most of whose conversation was about shooting. Soon I went mooning, more or less moodily, about the looming landscape, with its creaking-cowled hop-kilns and whirring flocks of starlings and hop-poles piled in pyramids like soldiers' tents. Often when I came home for five o'clock tea I felt a vague desire to be living somewhere else—in 1850, for example, when everything must have been so comfortable and old-fashioned, like the Cathedral Close in Trollope's novels. . . . There never seemed to be any reason for going to London, although, of course, there were interesting things to see there. (Aunt Evelyn was always intending to run up for the day and go to a matinee of Beerbohm Tree's new Shakespearean production.)

I seldom spoke to anyone while I was out for my walks, but now and again I would meet John Homeward, the carrier, on his way back from the county town where he went three days a week. Homeward was a friendly man: I always "passed the time of day" with him. He was a keen cricketer and one of Dixon's chief cronies. The weather and next year's cricket were the staple topics of our conversation. Homeward had been making his foot-pace journeys with his hooded van and nodding horse ever since I could remember, and he seemed an essential feature of the ten miles across the Weald to Ashbridge (a somnolent town which I associated with the smell of a brewery and the grim fact of people being hung in the gaol there). All the year round, whether there was snow on the ground or blossoms on the fruit trees, the carrier's van crawled across the valley with its cargo of utilities, but Homeward was always alone with his horse, for he never took passengers.

The summer was over and green months were discarded like garments for which I had no further use. Twiddling a pink second-class return ticket to London in my yellow-gloved fingers (old Miriam certainly had washed them jolly well) I stared through the carriage window at the early October landscape and ruminated on the opening meet in November. My excursions to London were infrequent, but I had an important reason for this one. I was going to try on my new hunting clothes and my new hunting boots. I had also got a seat for Kreisler's concert in the afternoon, but classical violin music was at present crowded out of my mind by the more urgent business of the day.

I felt as though I had an awful lot to do before lunch. Which had I better go to first, I wondered (jerking the window up as the train screeched into a tunnel), Craxwell or Kipward? To tell the truth I was a bit nervous about both of them; for when I had made my inaugural visits the individuals who patrolled the interiors of those eminent establishments had received me with such lofty condescension that I had begun by feeling an intruder. My clothes, I feared, had not been quite the cut and style that was expected of them by firms which had the names of reigning sovereigns on their books, and I was abashed by my ignorance of the specialized articles which I was ordering. Equilibrium of behaviour had perhaps been more difficult at the bootmaker's; so I decided to go to Kipward's first.

Emerging from Charing Cross I felt my personality somehow diluted. At Baldock Wood Station there had been no doubt that I was going up to town in my best dark blue suit, and London had been respectfully arranged at the other end of the line. But in Trafalgar Square my gentlemanly uniqueness had diminished to something almost nonentitive.

Had I been able to analyse my psychological condition I could have traced this sensation to the fact that my only obvious connections with the metropolis were as follows: Mr. Pennett in Lincoln's Inn Fields (he was beginning to give me up as a bad job) and the few shops where I owed money for books and clothes. No one else in London was aware of my existence. I felt half-inclined to go into the National Gallery, but there wasn't enough time for that. I had been to the British Museum once and the mere thought of it now made me feel bored and exhausted. Yet I vaguely knew that I ought to go to such places, in the same way that I knew I ought to read *Paradise Lost* and *The Pilgrim's Progress*. But there never seemed to be time for such edifications, and the Kreisler concert was quite enough for one day.

So I asserted my independence by taking a hansom to the tailor's, which was some distance along Oxford Street. I wasn't very keen on taxicabs, though the streets were full of them now.

The lower half of Kipward & Son's shop window was fitted with a fine wire screening, on which the crowns and vultures of several still

undethroned European Majesties were painted. In spite of this hauteur the exterior now seemed quite companionable, and I felt less of a nobody as I entered. A person who might well have been Mr. Kipward himself advanced to receive me; in his eyes there was the bland half-disdainful interrogation of a ducal butler; for the moment he still seemed uncertain as to my credentials. On the walls were some antlered heads and the whole place seemed to know much more about sport than I did. His suavely enunciated "what name?" made the butler resemblance more apparent, but with his, "Ah, yes, Mr. Sherston, of course; your coat and breeches are quite ready for you to try, sir," and the way he wafted me up a spacious flight of stairs, he became an old-fashioned innkeeper who had been in first-rate service,

and there seemed nothing in the world with which he was not prepared to accommodate me. To have asked the price of so much as a
waistcoat would have been an indecency. But I couldn't help wondering, as I was being ushered into one of the fitting compartments,
just how many guineas my black hunting-coat was going to cost.

A few minutes later I was sitting on a hard, shiny saddle and
being ciphered all over with a lump of chalk. The sallow little man
who fitted my breeches remarked that the buff Bedford cord which I
had selected was "a very popular one." As he put the finishing touch
with his chalk he asked me to stand up in the stirrups. Whereupon
he gazed upon his handiwork and found it good. "Yes, that's a beautiful seat," he remarked serenely. I wondered whether he would say
the same if he could see me landing over a post-and-rails on Harkaway. . . .

Stephen Colwood had advised me to patronize those particular
places, and it was no fault of his that I was still a comparative green-
horn.

Stopping at every station, a local train conveyed me sedately
into Sussex. Local and sedate, likewise, were the workings of my brain,
as I sat in an empty compartment with the *Southern Daily News* on
my knees. I had bought that unpretentious paper in order to read
about the Ringwell Hounds, whose doings were regularly reported
therein. And sure enough the previous day's sport was described in
detail. . . .

I allowed my thoughts to dally with the delightful prospect of
my being a participant in similar proceedings next day. Occasionally
I glanced affectionately at the bulging kit-bag containing those mas-
terpieces by Craxwell and Kipward which had cost me more than one
anxious journey to London. Would Stephen approve of my boots, I
wondered, staring out of the window at the reflective monochrome of
flooded meadows and the brown gloom of woodlands in the lowering
dusk of a heavily clouded December afternoon.

Whatever he might think of my boots, there was no doubt that
he approved of my arrival when the fussy little train stopped for the
last time and I found him waiting for me on the platform. I allowed

him to lug my bag out of the station, and soon he had got it stowed away in the old yellow-wheeled buggy, had flicked his father's favourite hunter into a trot ("a nailing good jumper, but as slow as a hearse"), and was telling me all about the clinking hunt they'd had the day before, and how he'd enjoyed my account of the Potford gallop. "You've got a regular gift for writing, you funny old cock! You might make a mint of money if you wrote for *Horse and Hound* or *The Field!*" he exclaimed, and we agreed that I couldn't write worse than the man in the *Southern Daily*, whose "Reynard then worked his way across the country" etc. afterwards became one of our stock jokes.

At nine o'clock next morning my cold fingers were making their usual bungling efforts to tie a white stock neatly; but as I had never been shown how to do it, my repeated failures didn't surprise me, though I was naturally anxious not to disgrace the Rectory on my first

appearance at a meet of the Ringwell Hounds. The breakfast bell was supplemented by Stephen's incitements to me to hurry up; these consisted in cries of "get-along-forrid" and similar hunt-servant noises, which accentuated my general feeling that I was in for a big day. While I was putting the final touches to my toilet I could hear him shouting to the two Scotch terriers who were scuttling about the lawn: (he was out there to have a look at that important thing, the weather).

Fully dressed and a bit flurried, I stumped downstairs and made for the low buzz of conversation in the dining-room. Purposing to make the moderately boisterous entry appropriate to a hunting morning, I opened the door. After a moment of stupefaction I recoiled into the passage, having beheld the entire household on its knees, with backs of varying sizes turned toward me: I had entered in the middle of the Lord's Prayer. After a temporizing stroll on the lawn I re-entered the room unobtrusively; Stephen handed me a plate of porridge with a grin and no other reference was made to my breach of decorum.

After breakfast he told me that I'd no more idea of tying a stock then an ironmonger; when he had re-tied it for me he surveyed the result with satisfaction and announced that I now "looked ready to compete against all the cutting and thrusting soldier-officers in creation."

By a quarter past ten the Rector was driving me to the meet in the buggy—the groom having ridden his horse on with Stephen, who was jogging sedately along on Jerry. The Rector, whose overcoat had an astrakhan collar, was rather reticent, and we did the five miles to the meet without exchanging many remarks. But it was a comfort, after my solitary sporting experiments, to feel that I had a couple of friendly chaperons, and Stephen had assured me that my hireling knew his way over every fence in the country and had never been known to turn his head. My only doubt was whether his rider would do him credit. We got to the meet in good time, and Mr. Whatman, a very large man who kept a very large livery-stable and drove a coach in the summer, was loquacious about the merits of my hireling, while he supervised my settlement in the saddle, which felt a hard and slippery one.

As I gathered up the thin and unflexible reins I felt that he was conferring a privilege on me by allowing me to ride the horse—a privilege for which the sum of thirty-five shillings seemed inadequate repayment. My mount was a wiry, nondescript-coloured animal, sober and unexcitable. It was evident from the first that he knew much more about the game than I did. He was what is known as a "safe conveyance" or "patent safety"; this more than atoned for his dry-coated and ill-groomed exterior. By the time I had been on his back an hour I felt more at home than I had ever done when out with the Dumborough.

The meet was at "The Five Bells," a wayside inn close to Basset Wood, which was the chief stronghold of fox preservation in that part of the Ringwell country. There was never any doubt about finding a fox at Basset. Almost a mile square, it was well-rided and easy to get about in, though none too easy to get a fox away from. It was also, as Stephen remarked when we entered it, an easy place to get left in unless one kept one's eyes and ears skinned. And his face kindled at the delightful notion of getting well away with the hounds, leaving three parts of the field coffee-housing at the wrong end of the covert. It was a grey morning, with a nip in the air which made him hopeful that "hounds would fairly scream along" if they got out in the open and, perhaps for the first time in my life, I felt a keen pleasure in the idea of sitting down and cramming my horse at every obstacle that might come in our way.

In the meantime I had got no more than a rough idea of the

seventy or eighty taciturn or chatting riders who were now making their way slowly along the main-ride while the huntsman could be heard cheering his hounds a little way off among the oaks and undergrowth. I had already noticed several sporting farmers in blue velvet caps and long-skirted black coats of country cut. And scarlet-coated Colonel Hesmon had proferred me a couple of brown-gloved fingers with the jaunty airified manner of a well-dressed absent-minded swell.

By the end of February I had made further progress in what I believed to be an important phase of my terrestrial experience. In other words (and aided by an exceptionally mild winter) I had averaged five days a fortnight with the hounds. I had, of course, confided in Dixon my intention of entering Cockbird for the Ringwell Heavy Weight Race. My main object now seemed to be to jump as many fences as possible before that eventful day arrived. Meets of the Dumborough had been disregarded, and a series of short visits to the Rectory had continued the "qualifying" of Cockbird. ("Qualifying" consisted in drawing the Master's attention to the horse during each day's

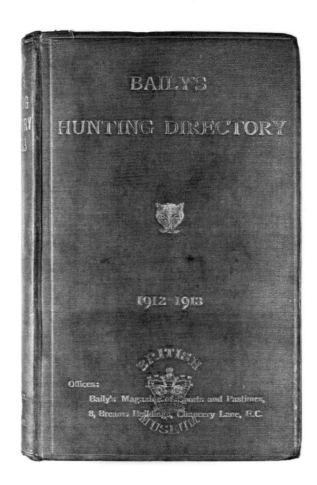

BAILY'S

HUNTING DIRECTORY

1912–1913

Offices:
Baily's Magazine of Sports and Pastimes,
8, Breams Buildings, Chancery Lane, E.C.

(1909). Ted Carroll; 2nd, Bert Savage. 50 couples of hounds, *unmarked.* Kennels—Elham, Canterbury. Telegraph Office and Railway Station—Elham (S.E.R.), ¼ mile. Days of Meetings—Monday, Wednesday, Friday and Saturday. Motors not objected to if halted at a reasonable distance rom the meet.

The country extends about 24 miles E. to W. and 18 miles from N. to S., in East Kent. On the N.W. it adjoins the Tickham; the sea lies on the S. and E. The fences are most frequently stake and binder, or post and rail; an occasional ditch or small brook in the vale country. About half is plough and woodland, the rest grass and downland. The grass increases every year. A certain amount of wire on the hills, but arrangements have been started to deal with it. There is an excellent piece of vale country called the Ashford Vale. A short-legged, active little horse is most suitable. Best centres: Canterbury, whence meets of the West Kent and Tickham are accessible; Folkestone and Dover.

The Master is guaranteed £1,100 yearly, with kennels, stables and Hunt servants' cottages rent free, and poultry fund. Minimum sub., £7 7s., and £2 2s. to Poultry and Damage Fund, is the minimum expected from those who hunt. Member's sub. at least £15 15s., and £3 3s. to P. and D. Fund; non-subscribers capped 10s. (1909). The hounds belong to the Country.

The Hunt probably dates from the 18th century, but records are wanting prior to Sir H. Oxenden's time.

Former Masters: Sir H. Oxenden, 1814—32. Mr. F. Brockman, 1832—70. The Earl of Guilford, 1870—79. Mr. F. J. Mackenzie, 1879—81. Mr. W. H. White, 1881—82. Mr. E. R. Sworder, 1882—89. Capt. F. Fitzroy, 1889—90. Mr. C. W. Prestcott-Westcar, 1890—93. Mr. A. B. Worthington, 1893—94. Mr. L. E. Bligh, 1894—98. Mr. Wilfrid Baker White, 1898—1900.

Veterinary Surgeons—Messrs. Crowhurst Brothers, Canterbury; Mr. Cooper, Dover.

Hotel—County Hotel, Canterbury: *see* Hotels for Sportsmen.

WEST KENT.

 Distinctive Collar—Black velvet, with white piping. Evening Dress—Scarlet, black velvet collar with silver piping, white facings, silver buttons. Master—(1910) C. B. Kidd, Esq., The Warren House, Otford, Kent. Hon. Secretary—(1911) W. M. Brydone, Red Lodge, Sevenoaks. Huntsman—(1912) The Master. Whippers-in—(1912) R. Easterby, (1912) S. Kinch. 45 couples of hounds, *marked* W. K. Kennels—Otford, near Sevenoaks. Telegraph Office and Railway Station—Otford (L.C. & D.R.). Days of Meeting—Tuesday, Thursday and Saturday.

The country covers about 17 miles by 17 in Kent. On the N. lies the River Thames; on the W. the Old Surrey; on the S. the Burstow and Eridge, and on the E. the Tickham. It is chiefly pasture, with a good deal of woodland and some plough. A short-legged horse is most suitable. Best centres, Farningham, Sevenoaks, Tonbridge, and Wrotham.

Minimum sub. £15 15s.; and two guineas to Damage Fund, a cap is taken. The hounds belong to the Hon. R. Nevill, C. A. Morris

Field, Esq., W. M. Cazalet, Esq., and C. B. Kidd, Esq., are lent by them to the Country.

The Hunt is one of very old establishment, Mr. John Warde, of Squerries, having hunted a good deal of the country from Westerham in 1776. In 1793 Sir John Dyke hunted the Bromley portion, another pack being kennelled at Sydenham. Sir Thomas Dyke, in succession to one or two members of his family, hunted the country till about 1830, the Hunt being known as the WEST KENT. In 1836 Mr. Forest took the country and kennelled his hounds at Greenhithe. Mr. Colyer succeeded him in 1845 (kennels at Milton, near Gravesend). Messrs. Armstrong and Wingfield Stratford as Joint Masters followed Mr. Colyer. Mr. Stratford resigned, and in 1858 Mr. Armstrong sold his hounds, Mr. Stratford buying about 15 couples, and hunting the country till 1861 or 1862, when he was joined by the Hon. R. Nevill. After this Joint Mastership came the following:—

Former Masters: Hon. R. P. Nevill, 1891. Col. C. Warde, M.P., 1891—92. Mr. R. Stewart-Saville, 1892—95. Lord George Nevill, 1895—1900. Mr. W. Baker-White, 1900—04. Mr. W. Gore Lambarde, 1904—08. Mr. R. Guy Everard, 1908—10.

Veterinary Surgeons—Mr. Percy Gregory, Tonbridge; Mr. Pugh, Sevenoaks.

Hotels—Royal Crown Hotel, Sevenoaks; County Hotel, Canterbury; *see* Hotels for Sportsmen.

LAMERTON.

 Distinctive Collar—Dark green. Evening Dress—Red, dark green facings, Hunt buttons. A Committee. Field Master and Hon. Secretary—A. C. Godfrey, Esq., Tavy Cottage, Tavistock. Huntsman—C. Woodridge. Whipper-in—W. Reddicliffe. 40 couples of hounds. Kennels—Stowford, Lewdown, N. Devon. Telegraph Office—Lewdown. Railway Station—Lifton (G.W.R.), 3 miles. Days of Meeting—Three days a week.

The country lies in Devon and Cornwall. On the N. it adjoins the Tetcott, Mr. Scott Browne's, and the Eggesford; on the W. the E. Cornwall; on the S. the Dartmoor, and on the E. the Mid-Devon. Pasture and moorland make up the country, which is one of big banks; on the moors are walls. Wire does not exist to an extent that gives trouble, and no arrangements are made to remove or mark it. A stout and clever horse that can jump big banks and get over rough moorland is required. Best centres, Tavistock, Launceston and Okehampton; from the last-named meets of the Eggesford and Mid-Devon can be reached.

No minimum sub. The subscription amounts to about £300 a year; no cap.

In 1840 the country was hunted in two parts, the N.W. portion by Mr. Archer, and the S.E. by Mr. Morgan. Mr. Phillips succeeded Mr. Archer about 1845; in 1853 Mr. H. Deacon bought Mr. Morgan's hounds and hunted the whole country until 1859, when he sold the hounds to the Hon. Mark Rolle. The twin brothers Leamon, who had previously kept harriers, then began to hunt foxes, and retained the Mastership until the death of Mr. Wm. Leamon in 1877.

Former Masters: Mr. H. Deacon, 1853—59. Mr. W. Leamon,

hunting; and I did this more than conscientiously, since Stephen and I were frequently shouted at by him for "larking" over fences when the hounds weren't running.)

The problem of Harkaway's lack of stamina had been solved by Dixon when he suggested that I should box him to the Staghound meets. He told me that they generally had the best of their fun in the first hour, so I could have a good gallop and bring the old horse home early. This took me (by a very early train from Baldock Wood) to a new and remote part of the country. . . .

The Coshford Vale Stag Hunt, which had been in existence as a subscription pack for about half a century, had been kept on its legs by the devoted efforts of a group of prosperous hop-farmers and a family of brewers whose name was a household word in the district. *Gimling's Fine Ales* were a passport to popularity, and the genial activities of Mr. "Gus" Gimling, who had been Master for more years than he cared to count, had kept the Hunt flourishing and assured it of a friendly reception almost everywhere in the country over which it hunted (described in the scarlet-covered Hunting Directory as "principally pasture with very little plough"). This description encouraged me to visualize an Elysium of green fields and jumpable hedges; but the country, although it failed to come up to my preconceived idea of its charms, included a nice bit of vale; and in those days there was very little wire in the fences.

· · ·

Provincial stag-hunts are commonly reputed to be comic and convivial gatherings which begin with an uproarious hunt-breakfast for the local farmers. Purple faced and bold with cherry brandy, they heave themselves on to their horses and set off across the country, frequently falling off in a ludicrous manner. But the Coshford sportsmen, as I knew them, were businesslike and well-behaved; they were out for a good old-fashioned gallop. In fact, I think of them as a somewhat serious body of men. And since the field was mainly composed of farmers, there was nothing smart or snobbish about the proceedings.

I need hardly say that there was no levity in my own attitude of mind when I set out for my first sample of this new experiment in sportsmanship. In spite of talking big to Dixon the night before, I felt more frightened than light-hearted. For I went alone and knew no one when I got there.

All through an extra fine summer I often wondered how the new Master was getting on in the Ringwell country. But I was almost entirely ignorant of what a Master of Hounds does with himself between April and September. I saw next to nothing of Stephen, who was at Aldershot, learning how to be a Special Reserve officer in the Royal Field Artillery.

My own energies were mainly expended on club cricket matches. I managed to play in three or four matches every week; I was intent on keeping my batting average up to twenty runs per innings, which I found far from easy, though I had one great afternoon when I compiled a century for Butley against some very mediocre village bowling. Those long days of dry weather and white figures moving to and fro on green grounds now seem like an epitome of all that was peaceful in my past. Walking home across the fields from Butley, or driving back in the cool of the evening after a high-scoring game on the county ground at Dumbridge, I deplored my own failure or gloated over one of my small successes; but I never looked ahead, except when I thought about next winter's hunting. The horses were out at grass; and so, in a sense, was I.

.   .   .

One week-end in July Stephen came to stay with us. Artillery life had caused no apparent change in him. We indulged in cheerful nostalgia for the chase. After sniffing the trussed hay in the stable-barn we contemplated Cockbird and Harkaway in the paddock. We sighed for a nice moist winter morning. Stephen was hoping to get "attached" to some Gunners who were conveniently stationed in the Ringwell country. He could tell me nothing about the new Master, except that he was already reputed to be a tireless worker and very well liked by the farmers. For his benefit I unearthed my early impression of Denis Milden as I had seen him when he was staying at Dumborough Castle as a boy. Already Milden was a very great man in our minds.

My memory of that summer returns like a bee that comes buzzing into a quiet room where the curtains are drawn on a blazing hot afternoon.

.   .   .

By the middle of September Dixon had got the horses up from grass. Cricket matches were out of season, but there hadn't been a spot of rain since the end of June. Robins warbled plaintively in our apple orchard, and time hung rather heavy on my hands. The Weald and the wooded slopes were blue misted on sultry afternoons when I was out for a ruminative ride on one of my indolent hunters. Hop-picking was over early that year and the merry pickers had returned to the slums of London to the strains of the concertina or accordion. I was contemplating an expedition to the West End to order a short-skirted scarlet coat and two pairs of white breeches from Kipward & Son; Craxwell was to make me a pair of boots with mahogany col-oured tops. I intended to blossom out at the opening meet as a full-fledged fox-hunter.

The autumn was a period of impatience. I longed for falling leaves and the first of November. The luminous melancholy of the fine September weather was a prelude rather than an elegy. I was only half in love with mists and mellow fruitfulness. I did not dread the dark winter as people do when they have lost their youth and live alone in some great city. Not wholly unconscious of the wistful splen-dour, but blind to its significance, I waited for cub-hunting to end.

Europe was nothing but a name to me. I couldn't even bring myself to read about it in the daily paper. I could, however, read about cubbing in the Midlands; it was described at some length every week in the columns of *Horse and Hound*.

Staying at the Kennels was the most significant occasion my little world could offer me, and in order that he might share my sublunary advancement I took Cockbird with me. In reply to my reserved little note I received a cheery letter from Denis: he would be delighted to see me and gave detailed instructions about my bag being called for and taken out to the Kennels from Downfield. He told me to be sure to bring a rug for my horse as he was "terrible short of clothing." My belongings were to be conveyed to the Kennels on the "flesh-cart," which would be in Downfield that day. I was surprised that he should take so much trouble, for I had yet to learn how methodical and thorough he was in everything which he undertook.

I remember nothing of that day's hunting; but the usual terse entry in my diary perpetuates the fact that the meet was at "The Barley Mow." "Found in Pilton Shaw and Crumpton Osiers, but did little with either as scent was rotten. Weather very wet in afternoon; had quite a good hunt of nearly two hours from Trodger's Wood; hounds were stopped in Basset Wood at 4.25." The concluding words, "Stayed at the Kennels," now seem a very bleak condensation of the event. But it did not occur to me that my sporting experiences would ever be called upon to provide material for a book, and I should have been much astonished if I could have foreseen my present efforts to put the clock back (or rather the calendar) from 1928 to 1911.

Yet I find it easy enough to recover a few minutes of that grey south-westerly morning, with its horsemen hustling on in scattered groups, the December air alive with the excitement of the chase, and the dull green landscape seeming to respond to the rousing cheer of the huntsman's voice when the hounds hit off the line again after a brief check. Away they stream, throwing up little splashes of water as they race across a half-flooded meadow. Cockbird flies a fence with a watery ditch on the take-off side. "How topping," I think, "to be alive and well up in the hunt"; and I spur along the sound turf of a

28

green park and past the front of a square pink Queen Anne house with blank windows and smokeless chimneys, and a formal garden with lawns and clipped yew hedges. . . . A stone statue stares at me, and I wonder who lived there when the house was first built. "I am riding past the past," I think, never dreaming that I shall one day write that moment down on paper; never dreaming that I shall be clarifying and condensing that chronicle of simple things through which I blundered so diffidently.

But the day's hunting is ended, and I must watch myself jogging back to the Kennels, soaked to the skin but quietly satisfied in my temporary embodiment in the Hunt establishment; beneath a clean-swept sky, too, for the rain-clouds have gone on with the wind behind them. Soon we are passing the village green; a quarter of a mile from the Kennels, Denis Milden blows a long wavering blast to warn the kennelman and the head-groom that we are almost home. When we turn in at a gate under some trees there are men waiting with swinging stable-lanterns, which flicker on their red jerseys, outside the long range of portable loose-boxes which Denis has put up. He and his whips are quickly off their horses and into the kennel-yard among the jostling hounds. He has told me to find my way indoors and get my tea and a bath. Cockbird is led into a loose-box under the superior eye of Meeston, the head-groom, a gruff, uncommunicative man in a long, dirty white kennel-coat. Cockbird gives his head a shake, glad to be rid of his bridle. Then he lowers it, and I pull his ears for a while—an operation which most horses enjoy when they are tired. The place is pervaded by a smell of oatmeal and boiled horse-flesh, and the vociferations of the hounds accompany me as I tread stiffly through the darkness to a wicket-gate, and so to the front door of the old wood-built huntsman's house—"the wooden hutch," as we used to call it.

An explanation of the continued prosperity of the Packlestone was largely to be found in Mrs. Oakfield of Thurrow Park, a lady who made friends wherever she went. Since her childhood she had been intimately associated with the Hunt, for her father had been Master for more than twenty years. From her large and well-managed estate she set an example of up-to-date (though somewhat expensive) farm-

management, and every farmer in the country (except a few stubborn Radicals) swore by Mrs. Oakfield as the feminine gender of a jolly good fellow. As a fine judge of cattle and sheep they respected her; and to this was added her reputation for boundless generosity. The Packlestone farmers were proud to see Mrs. Oakfield riding over their land—as well they might be, for it was a sight worth going a long way to see. A fine figure of a woman she was, they all agreed, as she sailed over the fences in her tall hat and perfectly fitting black habit with a bunch of violets in her buttonhole. This brilliant horsewoman rode over the country in an apparently effortless manner: always in the first flight, she never appeared to be competing for her prominent position; quick and dashing, she was never in a hurry; allowing for the fact that she was very well mounted and knew the country by heart, she was undoubtedly a paragon of natural efficiency. John Leech would have drawn her with delight. I admired Mrs. Oakfield enormously; her quickness to hounds was a revelation to me, and in addition she was gracious and charming in manner. Whether she bowed her acknowledgment to a lifted hat at the meet or cantered easily at an awkward bit of timber in an otherwise unjumpable hedge, she possessed the secret of style.

DURING THE SUMMER OF 1914 George Sherston had been thinking of horses and hunting instead of noticing the newspapers. Thus, as he says, his life "lumbered on into July, very much with the same sedate manner of progress which characterized Homeward's carrier's van." If he had been less dreamy he might have observed that on June 28 the Archduke Franz-Ferdinand, heir to the throne of Austria-Hungary, had been shot to death with his consort at Sarejevo in Bosnia, and that as a result Austria had declared war on Serbia, holding her responsible for this assassination. Mobilization and further declarations of war followed swiftly: Russia (allied with France) came to the support of Serbia, while Germany stood behind Austria-Hungary. By the end of July the situation was distinctly serious, and if George had been interested in the London news placards he would have read,

ALL EUROPE ARMING;
THE BRINK OF CATASTROPHE;
EUROPE DRIFTS TO DISASTER.

England was drawn in during the August Bank Holiday weekend. On Sunday, August 2, the German army entered Luxembourg, aiming at Paris by way of Belgium. On Monday the 3rd, England, allied by treaty with Belgium and by an "understanding" with France, presented Germany with an ultimatum: return home immediately or else. When the ultimatum expired at 11 o'clock at night on Tuesday, August 4th, the German army was advancing instead of withdrawing, and England was at war.

To the British the war was wildly popular because it seemed to be about honor and the sacredness of solemn international undertakings and the defense of small harmless countries like Belgium. Quickly military bands appeared in the streets, accompanied by broad banners reading, "We Are Marching to the Recruiting Station: JOIN US! Fall In Behind the Band." Within thirty days one of the best-known public images was the finger-pointing Lord Kitchener on posters above the words "Your Country Needs You." In the general enthusiasm more volunteers came forward than expected. They poured into unready camps where they shivered in bell tents during the winter. Drilling in civvies with sticks for rifles, they sang in mock-touching antiphony:

Where are our uniforms?
Far, far away.
When will our rifles come?
P'raps, p'raps some day.

And they were keen, anxious to become real soldiers as fast as possible. C. E. Montague remembers the spirit of these volunteers of 1914: "Real, constitutional lazy fellows would buy little cram-books of drill out of their

32

pay and sweat them up at night so as to get on the faster. Men warned for a guard next day would agree among themselves to get up an hour before the pre-dawn Réveillé to practice among themselves . . . in the hope of approaching the far-off, longed-for ideal of smartness, the passport to France." The opportunity of a wholesome, healthy life out-of-doors—that's what the war seemed to promise. And besides, it was going to be over in three months.

SITTING IN THE SUNSHINE one morning early in September, I ruminated on my five weeks' service as a trooper in the Yeomanry. Healthier than I'd ever been before, I sat on the slope of a meadow a few miles from Canterbury, polishing a cavalry saddle and wondering how it was that I'd never learned more about that sort of thing from Dixon. Below me, somewhere in the horse-lines, stood Cockbird, picketed to a peg in the ground by a rope which was already giving him a sore pastern. Had I been near enough to study his facial expression I should have seen what I already knew, that Cockbird definitely disliked being a trooper's charger. He was regretting Dixon and resenting mobilization. He didn't even belong to me now, for I had been obliged to sell him to the Government for a perfunctory fifty pounds, and I was lucky not to have lost sight of him altogether. Apart from the fact that for forty-five months he had been my most prized possession in the world, he was now my only tangible link with the peaceful past which had provided us both with a roof over our heads every night.

My present habitation was a bivouac, rigged up out of a rick-cloth and some posts, which I shared with eleven other troopers. Outside the bivouac I sat, with much equipment still uncleaned after our morning exercises. I had just received a letter, and it was lying on the grass beside me. It was from someone at the War Office whom I knew slightly; it offered me a commission, with the rank of captain, in the Remount Service. I had also got yesterday's *Times*, which contained a piece of poetry by Thomas Hardy. "What of the faith and fire within us, men who march away ere the barn-cocks say night is growing grey?" I did not need Hardy's "Song of the Soldiers" to warn me that the Remounts was no place for me. Also the idea of

SONG OF THE SOLDIERS.

What of the faith and fire within us
    Men who march away
    Ere the barn-cocks say
    Night is growing gray,
To hazards whence no tears can win us ;
What of the faith and fire within us
    Men who march away ?

Is it a purblind prank, O think you,
    Friend with the musing eye
    Who watch us stepping by,
    With doubt and dolorous sigh ?
Can much pondering so hoodwink you !
Is it a purblind prank, O think you,
    Friend with the musing eye ?

Nay.   We see well what we are doing,
    Though some may not see—
    Dalliers as they be !—
    England's need are we ;
Her distress would set us rueing :
Nay.   We see well what we are doing,
    Though some may not see !

In our heart of hearts believing
    Victory crowns the just,
    And that braggarts must
    Surely bite the dust,
March we to the field ungrieving,
In our heart of hearts believing
    Victory crowns the just.

Hence the faith and fire within us
    Men who march away
    Ere the barn-cocks say
    Night is growing gray,
To hazards whence no tears can win us ;
Hence the faith and fire within us
    Men who march away.
           THOMAS HARDY.

[*₊* Neither Mr. Hardy nor *The Times* reserves
copyright in the poem printed above.]

my becoming any sort of officer in the Army seemed absurd. I had already been offered a commission in my own Yeomanry, but how could I have accepted it when everybody was saying that the Germans might land at Dover any day? I was safe in the Army, and that was all I cared about.

I had slipped into the Downfield troop by enlisting two days before the declaration of war. For me, so far, the War had been a mounted infantry picnic in perfect weather. The inaugural excitement had died down, and I was agreeably relieved of all sense of personal responsibility. Cockbird's welfare was my main anxiety; apart from that, being in the Army was very much like being back at school. My incompetence, compared with the relative efficiency of my associates, was causing me perturbed and flustered moments. Getting on parade in time with myself and Cockbird properly strapped and buckled was ticklish work. But several of the officers had known me out hunting with the Ringwell, and my presence in the ranks was regarded as a bit of a joke, although in my own mind my duties were no laughing matter and I had serious aspirations to heroism in the field. Also I had the advantage of being a better rider than a good many of the men in my squadron, which to some extent balanced my ignorance and inefficiency in other respects.

The basis of my life with the "jolly Yeo-boys" was bodily fatigue, complicated by the minor details of my daily difficulties. There was also the uncertainty and the feeling of emergency which we shared with the rest of the world in that rumour-ridden conjuncture. But my fellow troopers were kind and helpful, and there was something almost idyllic about those early weeks of the War. The flavour and significance of life were around me in the homely smells of the thriving farm where we were quartered; my own abounding health responded zestfully to the outdoor world, to the apple-scented orchards, and all those fertilities which the harassed farmer was gathering in while stupendous events were developing across the Channel.

I had received a series of letters from Stephen, who was with an ammunition column on the Western Front and apparently in no immediate danger. He said there wasn't an honest jumpable fence in

Flanders; his forced optimism about next year's opening meet failed to convince me that he expected the "great contest," as he called it, to be over by then. Denis had disappeared into a cavalry regiment and was still in England. For him the world had been completely dis-integrated by the War, but he seemed to be making the best of a bad job.

It was five and a half months since I had been home. I had left Butley without telling anyone that I had made up my mind to enlist. On that ominous July 31st I said long and secret good-byes to every-thing and everyone. Late in a sultry afternoon I said good-bye to the drawing room. The sun-blinds (with their cords which tapped and creaked so queerly when there was any wind to shake them) were drawn down the tall windows; I was alone in the twilight room, with the glowering red of sunset peering through the chinks and casting the shadows of leaves on a fiery patch of light which rested on the wall by the photograph of "Love and Death." So I looked my last and rode away to the War on my bicycle. Somehow I knew that it was inevitable, and my one idea was to be first in the field. In fact, I made quite an impressive inward emotional experience out of it. It did not occur to me that everyone else would be rushing off to enlist next week. My gesture was, so to speak, an individual one, and I gloried in it.

I like to remember myself walking over one afternoon to consult Captain Huxtable about a commission in an infantry regiment. Captain Huxtable, who had always shown an almost avuncular concern for my career, had joined the Army in 1860. He was a brisk, freckled, God-fearing, cheerful little man, and although he was now over seventy, he didn't seem to have altered in appearance since I was a child. He was a wonderful man for his age. Chairman of the local bench, churchwarden, fond of a day's shooting with Squire Maundle, comfortably occupied with a moderate sized farm overlooking the Weald, he was a pattern of neighbourly qualities, and there was no one with whom Aunt Evelyn more enjoyed a good gossip. Time-honoured jokes passed between them, and his manner toward her was jovial, spruce, and gallant. He was a neat skater, and his compact homespun figure seemed to find its most appropriate setting when the ponds froze and he was cutting his neat curves on the hard, ringing surface; his apple-cheeked countenance, too, had a sort of blithe good-humour which seemed in keeping with fine frosty weather. He was a man who knew a good Stilton cheese and preferred it over ripe. His shrewd and watchful eyes had stocked his mind with accurate knowledge of the countryside. He was, as he said himself, "addicted to observing the habits of a rook," and he was also a keen gardener.

Captain Huxtable was therefore an epitome of all that was most pleasant and homely in the countrified life for which I was proposing to risk my own. And so, though neither of us was aware of it, there was a grimly jocular element in the fact that it was to him that I

turned for assistance. It may be inferred that he had no wish that I should be killed, and that he would have been glad if he could have gone to the Front himself, things being as they were; but he would have regarded it as a greater tragedy if he had seen me shirking my responsibility. To him, as to me, the War was inevitable and justifiable. Courage remained a virtue. And that exploitation of courage, if I may be allowed to say a thing so obvious, was the essential tragedy of the War, which, as everyone now agrees, was a crime against humanity.

It is ten years since I uttered an infantry word of command: and I am only one of a multitude of men in whose minds parade ground phraseology has become as obsolete and derelict as a rusty kettle in a ditch. So much so that it seems quite illuminating to mention the fact. "At the halt on the left form platoon" now sounds to me positively peculiar, and to read *Infantry Training 1914* for a few minutes might be an almost stimulating experience. Though banished to the

PART III.

GENERAL REMARKS.

A Platoon Commander will have gone a long way towards having a well-trained platoon if he has gained the confidence of his N.C.O.s and men and has established a high soldierly spirit in all ranks.

The confidence of his men can be gained by:—

(a) Being the best man at arms in the platoon, or trying to be so;

(b) Being quick to act, taking real command on all occasions, issuing clear orders, and not forgetting to see them carried out;

(c) Example, being himself well turned out, punctual, and cheery, even under adverse circumstances;

(d) Enforcing strict discipline at all times. This must be a willing discipline, not a sulky one. Be just, but do not be soft—men despise softness.

(e) Recognising a good effort, even if it is not really successful. A word of praise when deserved produces better results than incessant fault-finding;

(f) Looking after his men's comfort before his own and never sparing himself;

(g) Demanding a high standard on all occasions, and never resting content with what he takes over, be it on the battlefield or in billets. Everything is capable of improvement, from information on the battlefield down to latrines and washing places in billets;

(h) Being blood-thirsty, and for ever thinking how to kill the enemy, and helping his men to do so.

The Platoon Commander should be the proudest man in the Army. He is the Commander of *the* unit in the attack. He is the only Commander who can know intimately the character and capabilities of each man under him. He can, if he is so disposed, establish an esprit de platoon which will be hard to equal in any other formation.

backs of our minds, those automatic utterances can still be recalled; but who can restore Clitherland Camp and its counterparts all over the country? Most of them were constructed on waste land; and to waste land they have relapsed. I cannot imagine any ex-soldier revisiting Clitherland in pensive pilgrimage.

. . .

Unrolling my valise in a comfortless hut on that first afternoon, I was completely cut off from anything I had done before. Not a soul in the Camp had ever set eyes on me until to-day. And I was totally ignorant of all that I had to learn before I was fit to go to the Front. Fixing up my folding bed, in which I managed to pinch my finger, I listened to what this new world had to tell me. A bugle call was blown—rather out of tune—but what event it signalized I couldn't say. An officer's servant was whistling cheerfully, probably to a pair of brown shoes. A door banged and his army boots thumped hastily along the passage. Then a sedate tread passed along on the boards, evidently some senior officer. Silence filled a gap, and then I heard a dusty rhythm of marching feet; the troops were returning from the drill-field up the road. Finally, from the open space behind the officers' quarters, a manly young voice shouted: "At the halt on the left form close column of platoons." Clitherland Camp had got through another afternoon parade. I was in a soldier manufactory, although I did not see it that way at the time.

. . .

It must not be assumed that I found life in the Camp at all grim and unpleasant. Everything was as aggressively cheerful and alert as the ginger-haired sergeant-major who taught the new officers how to form fours and slope arms, and so on, until they could drill a company of recruits with rigid assurance. In May, 1915, the recruits were men who had voluntarily joined up, the average age of the second lieutenants was twenty-one, and "war-weariness" had not yet been heard

of. I was twenty-eight myself, but I was five years younger in looks, and in a few days I was one of this outwardly light-hearted assortment, whose only purpose was to "get sent out" as soon as possible.

. . .

The Colonel probably took it as all in the day's work when he toddled out after mess on some night when a draft was "proceeding to the Front." Out on the Square he would find, perhaps, 150 men drawn up; discipline would be none too strict, since most of them had been fortifying themselves in the canteen. He would make his stuttering little farewell speech about being a credit to the regiment; going out to the Big Push which will end the War; and so on. And then the local clergyman would exhort them to trust in their Saviour, to an accompaniment of asides and witticisms in Welsh.

"And now God go with you," he would conclude, adding, "I will go with you as far as the station. . . ."

And they would march away in the dark, singing to the beat of drums. It wasn't impressive, but what else could the Colonel and the clergyman have said or done?

. . .

THE DEGREE TO WHICH Sassoon is fictionalizing is well illustrated in the passage that follows. "Stephen Colwood" is based on Sassoon's friend Gordon Harbord, who was actually killed August 14, 1917, more than two years after Stephen is killed here. Sassoon has moved his death forward so that it occurs in proximity to Dick Tiltwood, supplying meaning retroactively to the earlier mention of Watts's painting Love and Death. By this means Sassoon also avoids the inconvenience of equipping Sherston with two ideal companions at one time.

Sassoon's methods for naming his characters can be inferred from his transformation of Gordon Harbord into Stephen Colwood. In the London Times for August 21, 1917, this casualty notice appears:

> HARBORD.–Killed in action, on the 14th August. Lt. (Temp. Capt.) Stephen Gordon Harbord, M.C., R.F.A., third son of Rev. H. and Mrs. Harbord, Colwood Park, Bolney. Aged 27.

SOME NEW OFFICERS arrived, and one of them took the place of the silent civil-engineer in my room. We had the use of the local cricket-ground; I came in that evening feeling peaceful after batting and bowling at the nets for an hour. It seemed something to be grateful for—that the War hadn't killed cricket yet, and already it was a relief to be in flannels and out of uniform. Coming cheerfully into the hut I saw my new companion for the first time. He had unpacked and arranged his belongings, and was sitting on his camp-bed polishing a perfectly new pipe. He looked up at me. Twilight was falling and there was only one small window, but even in the half-light his face surprised me by its candour and freshness. He had the obvious good looks which go with fair hair and firm features, but it was the radiant integrity of his expression which astonished me. While I was getting ready for dinner we exchanged a few remarks. His tone of voice was simple and reassuring, like his appearance. How does he manage to look like that? I thought; and for the moment I felt all my age, though the world had taught me little enough, as I knew then, and know even better now. His was the bright countenance of truth; ignorant and undoubting; incapable of concealment but strong in reticence and modesty. In fact, he was as good as gold, and everyone knew it as soon as they knew him.

Such was Dick Tiltwood, who had left school six months before and had since passed through Sandhurst. He was the son of a parson with a good family living. Generations of upright country gentlemen had made Dick Tiltwood what he was, and he had arrived at manhood in the nick of time to serve his country in what he naturally assumed to be a just and glorious war. Everyone told him so; and when he came to Clitherland Camp he was a shining epitome of his unembittered generation which gladly gave itself to the German shells and machine-guns—more gladly, perhaps, than the generation which knew how much (or how little, some would say) it had to lose. Dick made all the difference to my life at Clitherland. Apart from his cheerful companionship, which was like perpetual fine weather, his Sandhurst training enabled him to help me in mine. Patiently he heard me while I went through my repetitions of the mechanism of the rifle. And in company drill, which I was slow in learning, he was equally helpful. In return for this I talked to him about fox-hunting, which never failed to interest him. He had hunted very little, but he regarded it as immensely important, and much of the material of these memoirs became familiar to him through our conversations in the hut: I used to read him Stephen's letters from the Front, which were long and full of amusing references to the sport that for him symbolized everything enjoyable which the War had interrupted and put an end to. His references to the War were facetious. "An eight-inch landed and duly expanded this morning twenty yards from our mess, which was half-filled with earth. However, the fourth footman soon cleared it and my sausage wasn't even cracked, so I had quite a good breakfast." . . . Dick got to know Stephen quite well, although he had never seen him, except in a little photograph I had with me. So we defied the boredom of life in the Camp, and while the summer went past us our only fear was that we might be separated when our turn came to go abroad. He gave me a sense of security, for his smooth head was no more perplexed with problems than a robin redbreast's; he wound up his watch, brushed his hair, and said his prayers morning and evening.

September arrived, and we were both expecting to get a week's leave. (It was known as "last leave.") One morning Dick came into the hut with a telegram which he handed me. It happened that I was orderly officer that day. Being orderly officer meant a day of dull perfunctory duties, such as turning out the guard, inspecting the prisoners in the guardroom, the cookhouses, the canteen, and everything else in the Camp. When I opened my telegram the orderly sergeant was waiting outside for me; we were due for a tour of the men's huts while they were having their mid-day meal. The telegram was signed Colwood; it informed me that Stephen had been killed in action. But the orderly sergeant was waiting, and away we went, walking briskly over the grit and gravel. At each hut he opened the door and shouted "Shun!" The clatter and chatter ceased and all I had to ask was "Any complaints?" There were no complaints, and off we went to the next hut. It was queer to be doing it, with that dazed feeling and the telegram in my pocket. . . . I showed Dick the telegram when I returned. I had seen Stephen when he was on leave in the spring, and he had written to me only a week ago. Reading the Roll of Honour in the daily paper wasn't the same thing as this. Looking at Dick's blank face I became aware that he would never see Stephen now, and the meaning of the telegram became clear to me.

Dick and I were on our way to the First Battalion. The real War, that big bullying bogey, had stood up and beckoned to us at last; and now the Base Camp was behind us with its overcrowded discomforts that were unmitigated by *esprit de corps*. . . . For the first time in our lives we had crossed the Channel. We had crossed it in bright moonlight on a calm sea—Dick and I sitting together on a tarpaulin cover in the bow of the boat, which was happily named *Victoria*.

It felt funny to be in France for the first time. The sober-coloured country all the way from Etaples had looked lifeless and unattractive, I thought. But one couldn't expect much on a starved grey November morning. A hopeless hunting country, it looked. . . . The opening meet would have been last week if there hadn't been this war. . . . Dick was munching chocolate and reading the *Strand Magazine*, with its cosy reminder of London traffic on the cover. I hadn't lost sight of *him* yet, thank goodness. The Adjutant at Clitherland had sworn

to do his best to get us both sent to the First Battalion. But it was probably an accident that he had succeeded. It was a lucky beginning, anyhow. What a railway-tasting mouth I'd got! A cup of coffee would be nice, though French coffee tasted rather nasty, I thought. . . . We got to Béthune by half-past ten.

.   .   .

For the time being the Western Front received us into comparative comfort and domesticity. We found Captain Barton, the company commander, by a stove (which was smoking badly) in a small tiled room on the ground floor of a small house on the road from Béthune to Festubert. The smoke made my eyes water, but otherwise things were quite cheerful. We all slept on the floor, the hardness and coldness of which may be imagined. But then, as always, my sleeping-bag (or "flea-bag" as we called it) was a good friend to me, and we were in clover compared with the men (no one who was in the War need be reminded of that unavoidable circumstance).

Barton (like all the battalion officers except the C.O., the second-in-command, and the quartermaster, and four or five subalterns from Sandhurst) was a civilian. He was big, burly, good-natured, and easy-going; had been at Harrow and, until the War, had lived a comfortably married life on an adequate unearned income. He was, in fact, a man of snug and domesticated habits and his mere presence (wearing pince-nez) in a front-line trench made one feel that it *ought*, at any

45

rate, to be cosy. Such an inherently amicable man as Barton was a continual reminder of the incongruity of war with everyday humanity. In the meantime he was making gallant efforts to behave professionally, and keep his end up as a company commander.

. . .

So my company received me: and for an infantry subaltern the huge unhappy mechanism of the Western Front always narrowed down to the company he was in. My platoon accepted me apathetically. It was a diminished and exhausted little platoon, and its mind was occupied with anticipations of "Divisional Rest."

To revert to my earlier fact, "got to Béthune by half-past ten," it may well be asked how I can state the time of arrival so confidently. My authority is the diary which I began to keep when I left England. Yes; I kept a diary, and intend to quote from it (though the material which it contains is meagre). But need this be amplified? . . .

"*Thursday.* Went on working-party, 3 to 10.30 p.m. Marched to Festubert, a ruined village, shelled to bits. About 4.30, in darkness and rain, started up half a mile of light-railway lines through marsh,

with sixty men. Then they carried hurdles up the communication trenches, about three-quarters of a mile, which took two hours. Flares went off frequently; a few shells, high overhead, and exploding far behind us. The trenches are very wet. Finally emerged at a place behind the first- and second-line trenches, where new trenches (with 'high-command breastworks') are being dug.

"*Saturday*. Working-party again. Started 9.45 p.m. in bright moonlight and iron frost. Dug 12-2. Men got soup in ruined house in Festubert, with the moon shining through matchwood skeleton rafters. Up behind the trenches, the frost-bound morasses and ditches and old earthworks in moonlight, with dusky figures filing across the open, hobbling to avoid slipping. Home 4.15.

"*Sunday*. Same as Saturday. Dug 12-2. Very cold.

"*Monday*. Went with working-party at 3 p.m. Wet day. Awful mud. Tried to dig, till 7.30, and came home soaked. Back 9.45. Beastly night for the men, whose billets are wretched."

I can see myself coming in, that last night, with Julian Durley, a shy, stolid-faced platoon commander who had been a clerk in

47

Somerset House. He took the men's discomforts very much to heart. Simple and unassertive, he liked sound literature, and had a sort of metropolitan turn of humour. His jokes, when things were going badly, reminded me of a facetious bus conductor on a wet winter day. Durley was an inspiration toward selfless patience. He was an ideal platoon officer, and an example which I tried to imitate from that night onward. I need hardly say that he had never hunted. He could swim like a fish, but no social status was attached to that.

When I had been with the battalion a week we moved away from the La Bassée sector at nine o'clock on a fine bright morning. In spite of my quite mild experiences there, I felt that I'd seen more than enough of that part of the country. Barton and Durley and young Ormand (who was now second-in-command of the company) were always talking about the Givenchy trenches and how their dugout had been "plastered with trench-mortars and whizz-bangs." Now that they were out of it they seemed to take an almost morbid delight in remembering their escapes. No one knew where we were moving to, but the Quartermaster had told Barton that we might be going

south. "New Army" battalions were beginning to arrive in France, and the British line was being extended.

On our second day's march (we had done ten kilometres to a comfortable billet the first day) we passed an infantry brigade of Kitchener's Army. It was raining; the flat dreary landscape was half-hidden by mist, and the road was liquid mud. We had fallen out for a halt when they passed us. Four after four they came, some of them wearing the steel basin-helmets which were new to the English armies then. The helmets gave them a Chinese look. To tell the truth, their faces looked sullen, wretched, and brutal as they sweated with the packs under glistening waterproof capes. Worried civilian officers on horses, young-looking subalterns in new rainproof trench-coats; and behind the trudging column the heavy transport horses plodding through the sludge, straining at their loads, and the stolid drivers munching, smoking, grinning, yelling coarse gibes at one another. It was the War all right, and they were going in the direction of it.

While riding alone I explored the country rather absentmindedly, meditating on the horrors which I had yet to experience; I was unable to reconcile that skeleton certainty with the serenities of this winter landscape—clean-smelling, with larks in the sky, the rich brown gloom of distant woods, and the cloud shadows racing over the lit and dappled levels of that widespread land. And then I would pass a grey-roofed château, with its many windows and no face there to watch me pass . . . , the whole place forlorn and deserted.

POISON GAS, although its tendency to drift back on its deployers made it not as effective as hoped, gained some vogue as an offensive weapon in a war where nothing else seemed to work as well as it was supposed to either. Gas was first used in April 1915 when the Germans supported an attack of theirs at Ypres by squirting chlorine gas out of cylinders. At Loos in September 1915 the British retaliated: they prepared to attack by discharging gas across No Man's Land for forty minutes, but unfortunately they did so in a dead calm, the gas drifting back into their own positions with disastrous results.

As each side tried to master the offensive use of gas, it labored to develop defensive masks. They grew in sophistication as the war went on. "The first respirator issued in France," says Robert Graves in Good-Bye to All That, "was a gauze-pad filled with chemically-treated cotton waste, for tying across the mouth and nose. Reputedly it could not keep out the German gas, . . . but we never put it to the test. A week or two later came the 'smoke-helmet,' a greasy grey-felt bag with a talc window to look through, but no mouthpiece, certainly ineffective against gas. The talc was always cracking, and visible leaks showed at the stitches joining it to the helmet." Finally came another version, mentioned here by Sassoon, which Graves says was "popularly known as 'the goggle-eyed booger with the tit.' It differed from the previous models. One breathed in through the nose from inside the helmet, and breathed out through a special valve held in the mouth." The yet-to-be-devised final version, the more familiar "box respirator," consisted of a rubber and fabric face-piece and breathing tube running down to a canister of chemicals carried in a breast pack. It was more or less effective, much more serious than the early improvisations run up by ladies at home, as described by Mrs. C. S. Peel: "At one moment there was an S.O.S. for workers to make gas masks. We hurried to obey, and sewed up some sort of strange contraption composed chiefly of black net. Thousands of them—perfectly useless, it was afterwards declared—were made. What became of them?"

EARLY IN THE New Year the first gas-masks were issued. Every morning we practised putting them on, transforming ourselves into grotesque goggle-faced creatures as we tucked the grey flannel under our tunics in flustered haste. Those masks were an omen. An old wood-cutter in leather leggings watched us curiously, for we were doing our gas-drill on the fringe of the forest, with its dark cypresses among the leafless oaks and beeches, and a faint golden light over all.

On Sunday in January I got leave to go into Amiens. (A rambling train took an hour and a half to do the eighteen-mile journey.) Dick went with me. After a good lunch we inspected the Cathedral, which was a contrast to the life we had been leading. But it was crowded with sight-seeing British soldiers; the kilted "Jocks" walked up and down the nave as if they had conquered France, and I remember seeing a Japanese officer flit in with curious eyes. The long capes which many of the soldiers wore gave them a medieval aspect, insolent and overbearing. But the background was solemn and beautiful. White columns soared into lilies of light, and the stained-glass windows harmonized with the chanting voices and the satisfying sounds of the organ. I glanced at Dick and thought what a young Galahad he looked (a Galahad who had got his school colours for cricket).

Pushing past the gas-blanket, I blundered down the stairs to the company headquarters' dug-out. There were twenty steps to that earthy smelling den, with its thick wooden props down the middle and its precarious yellow candlelight casting wobbling shadows. Barton was sitting on a box at the rough table, with a tin mug and a half-

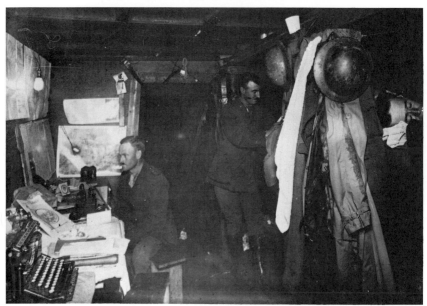

52

empty whisky bottle. . . . Dick was in deep shadow, lying on a bunk (made of wire-netting with empty sandbags on it). It was a morose cramped little scene, loathsome to live in as it is hateful to remember. The air was dank and musty; lumps of chalk fell from the "ceiling" at intervals. There was a bad smell of burnt grease, and the frizzle of something frying in the adjoining kennel that was called the kitchen was the only evidence of ordinary civilization—that and Barton's shining pince-nez, and the maps and notebooks which were on the table.

REMEMBERING SASSOON'S "Dick Tiltwood," Graves writes in Good-Bye to All That:

"One evening . . . Richardson, David Thomas and I met Pritchard and the Adjutant. We stopped to talk. Richardson complained what a devil of a place this was for trench-mortars. . . .

"The Adjutant said, 'We've had three hundred casualties in the last month here. It doesn't seem so many as that because, curiously enough, none of them have been officers. In fact we've had about five hundred casualties in the ranks since Loos, and not a single officer.'

"Then he suddenly realized that his words were unlucky.

" 'Touch wood!' David cried. Everybody jumped to touch wood, but it was a French trench and unrevetted. I pulled a pencil out of my pocket; that was wood enough for me. . . .

"The following evening I led 'A' Company forward as a working-party. 'B' and 'D' Companies were in the line, and we overtook 'C' also going to work. David, bringing up the rear of 'C', looked worried about something. 'What's wrong?' I asked.

" 'Oh, I'm fed up,' he answered, 'and I've got a cold.' . . .

" 'A' Company worked from seven in the evening until midnight. We must have put three thousand sandbags into position, and fifty yards of front trench were already looking presentable. About half-past ten, rifle-fire broke out on the right, and the sentries passed along the news: 'Officer hit.'

"Richardson hurried away to investigate. He came back to say: 'It's young Thomas. A bullet through the neck; but I think he's all right. It can't have hit his spine or an artery, because he's walking to the dressing-station.'

"I was delighted: David should now be out of it long enough to escape the coming offensive, and perhaps even the rest of the War. . . .

"Then news came that David was dead. The Regimental doctor, a throat specialist in civil life, had told him at the dressing-station: 'You'll be all right, only don't raise your head for a bit.' David then took a letter from his pocket, gave it to an orderly, and said: 'Post this!' It had been written to a girl in Glamorgan, for delivery if he got killed. The doctor saw that he was choking and tried tracheotomy; but too late. . . .

"I felt David's death worse than any other since I had been in France, but it did not anger me as it did Siegfried. He was Acting Transport Officer, and every evening now, when he came up with the rations, went out on patrol looking for Germans to kill. I just felt empty and lost."

COMING UP FROM the transport lines at twelve o'clock next morning I found Joe Dottrell standing outside the Quartermaster's stores. His face warned me to expect bad news. No news could have been worse. Dick had been killed. He had been hit in the throat by a rifle bullet while out with the wiring-party, and had died at the dressing-station a few hours afterwards. The battalion doctor had been a throat specialist before the War, but this had not been enough.

The sky was angry with a red smoky sunset when we rode up with the rations. Later on, when it was dark, we stood on the bare slope just above the ration dump while the Brigade chaplain went through his words; a flag covered all that we were there for; only the white stripes on the flag made any impression on the dimness of the night. Once the chaplain's words were obliterated by a prolonged burst of machine-gun fire; when he had finished, a trench-mortar "canister" fell a few hundred yards away, spouting the earth up with a crash. . . . A sack was lowered into a hole in the ground. The sack was Dick. I knew Death then.

Easter was late in April that year; my first three tours of trenches occupied me during the last thirty days of Lent. This essential season in the Church calendar was not, as far as I remember, remarked upon by anyone in my company, although the name of Christ was often on

54

ROLL OF HONOUR.

110 CASUALTIES TO OFFICERS.

42 REPORTED DEAD.

The Secretary of the Admiralty announces the following casualties :—

KILLED, MARCH 23.
Irvine, Lieut. James, R.N.R.
Thornton, Mr. Frank E., Skipper, R.N.R.

DIED, MARCH 23.
Herewyt de Bless, Midshipman Gervase A. D., R.N.

DIED, MARCH 24.
Rotherham, Lieut. Donald K., R.N.

INJURED, MARCH 24.
Bush, Flight Sub.-Lt. R. E., R.N.

EXPEDITIONARY FORCE.

Expeditionary Force, reported from General Headquarters, under date March 19 :—

KILLED.
Clow, Sec. Lt. G. R., 9th Black Watch.
Howard, Sec. Lieut. R. J., 10th, attd. 9th, Black Watch.
Marshall, Capt. F., 24th (Oldham) Manchester Regt.
Sheepshanks, Lt. C. J. H., 8th Devon Regt.
Stephenson, Sec. Lt. E. L., 4th (T.F.) Lincoln Regt.
Stoer, Sec. Lt. F. C., 6th Duke of Cornwall's L.I.

DIED OF WOUNDS.
Crabb, Sec. Lt. T. H., 4th R. Fusiliers.
Macdonald, Capt. J. D., Graves Registration Commission.
Mather, Sec. Lt. C. H., 12th Northumberland Fus.
Robinson, Lt. L. H. F., 7th E. Surrey Regt.

WOUNDED.
Andrews, Capt. J. A., 2nd Devon Regt.
Bowers, Sec. Lt. J. F. F., 10th Highland L.I.
Davenport, Sec. Lt. S. E., 8th R. Berks Regt.
Gascoyne, Sec. Lt. W. L., 9th, attd. 8th, R. W. Kent Regt.
Getty, Sec. Lt. J. B., 17th, attd. 2nd, R. Irish Rifles.
Hardie, Sec. Lt. E. E., 3rd, attd. 2nd, Gordon Highrs.
Heather, Maj. V. J., R. Field Artillery.
Keith, Lt. J., 10th, attd. 8th, Seaforth Highrs.
Kirton, Sec. Lt. R. I., K. O. Scottish Bordrs. and R. Flying Corps.
Lindsay, Sec. Lt. D. C. M., 3rd, attd. 1st, Black Watch.
Macmillan, Sec. Lt. C., 8th Seaforth Highrs.
Moss, Lt. W. P., 3rd, attd. 2nd, R. Irish Rifles.
Myles, Capt. J. F., 8th Seaforth Highrs.
Russell, Sec. Lt. J., 26th (3rd Tyneside Irish) Northumberland Fus.
Scott, Sec. Lt. J., 5th Cameron Highrs.
Simmins, Sec. Lt. S. G., 10th, attd. 7th, R. Sussex Regt.
Smith, Lt. N. V., 12th Durham L.I.
Warnington, Sec. Lt. C., 6th E. Kent Regt.
Wintle, Sec. Lt. A. L. C., 9th (Co. Tyrone), R. Inniskilling Fus.
Young, Capt. V. L., 6th (T.F.) Gloucester Regt.

Expeditionary Force, reported from General Headquarters under date March 20 :—

KILLED.
Burnell, Capt. A. C., 2nd Rifle Brigade.
Edwards, Capt. P. A., 1st L. N. Lancs Regt.
McWilliam, Lt. C. T., 5th (Buchan and Formartin) (T.F.) Gordon Highrs., attd. Highland Divl. Cyclist Co., Div. Mtd. Troops (T.F.).
Pearson, Sec. Lt. C. H., 6th (T.F.) South Stafford Regt.
Radcliffe, Lt. D., 24th (2nd Sportsman's) R. Fusiliers.
Standen, Lt. L. J. D., 5th (T.F.) Lincoln Regt.
White, Lt. L., 10th (1st Rhondda) Welsh Regt.

DIED OF WOUNDS.
Fairweather, Lt. L. J. E. C., 3rd, attd. 8th, Lincoln Regt.
Richardson, Capt. M. S., 1st R. Welsh Fus.
Thomas, Sec. Lt. D. O., 3rd, attd. 1st, R. Welsh Fus.

WOUNDED.
Beveridge, Sec. Lt. G., 7th (Deeside Highland) (T.F.)

King, Sec. Lt. T. C., 1st Middlesex Regt.
McClure, Sec. Lt. J. R. S., R. Engineers.
Mackay, Sec. Lt. S., 8th Northampton Regt.
McLean, Sec. Lt. A. E. J., 9th King's R. Rifle Corps.
Page, Capt. H. A., 6th (T.F.) S. Stafford Regt.
Price, Lt. E. D., 3rd, attd 2nd, R. Irish Regt.
Rice, Sec. Lt. G. H., R. Engineers.
Rogerson, Capt. A. W., 8th (Argyllshire) (T.F.) Argyll and Sutherland Highrs., attd. Army Cyclist Corps.
Smith, Lt. G. H., 6th (T.F.) S. Stafford Regt.
Stevens, Sec. Lt. A. R. I., 9th R. Fusiliers.
Stoop, Lt. F. M., 7th E. Kent Regt.
Tapp, Sec. Lt. G. N., 14th Cheshire Regt., attd. 2nd Yorkshire L.I.
Tolley, Sec. Lt. W. E., 3rd, attd. 2nd, Lincoln Regt.

MISSING.
Burnley, Sec. Lt. C. P., 8th R. W. Surrey Regt.
Expeditionary Force, reported under various dates :—
Previously reported Missing, Believed Killed, now reported Killed.
Plant, Sec. Lt. F. G., 1st R. W. Surrey Regt.
Previously reported Missing, now reported Killed.
Bosworth, Sec. Lt. A. W., 8th Lincoln Regt.
Macrae, Sec. Lt. F. L., 8th Seaforth Highrs.

WOUNDED.
Allen, Rev. H. D., Army Chaplains' Dept.
Hambro, Brigadier-General P. O.

Canadian Contingent with the Expeditionary Force, reported under various dates :—

DIED OF WOUNDS.
Bates, Maj. W., 25th Canadian Inf. Bn.

WOUNDED.
Davis, Lt. W. W., 2nd Canadian Pioneer Bn.
Delancey, Lt. J. A., 25th Canadian Inf. Bn.
Dorval, Lt. C. O., 22nd Canadian Inf. Bn.
Lewis, Lt. J. T., 2nd Canadian Divl. Signal Co.

THE INDIAN FORCES.

The Indian Forces, reported under various dates :—

EXPEDITIONARY FORCE.

DIED.
Teesdale, Maj. F. R., 25th Cavalry Brigade Staff.

EAST AFRICA.

KILLED.
Wilson, Lt. R. E., Bombay Volunteer Rifles.

MESOPOTAMIA.

KILLED.
Ganga Singh, Subadar, 53rd Sikhs.
Kapur Singh, Jemadar, 53rd Sikhs.
Khawas Shah, Jemadar, Guides Infantry, attd. 24th Punjabis.
Muzaffaruddin, Ahmad Ressaidar, 4th Cavalry.
Nawal Singh, Jemadar, 97th Infantry.
Suhan Singh, Jemadar, 47th Sikhs.
Surat Singh, Subadar, 53rd Sikhs.

DIED.
Hebbert, Capt. R. F., Indian Medical Service.

DIED OF WOUNDS.
Nur Khan, Subadar, 53rd Sikhs.

WOUNDED.
Baryam Singh, Bahadur, I.O.M., Subadar, 3rd Sappers and Miners.
Bhagwan Singh, Subadar, 97th Infantry.
Chittar Singh, Subadar, 122nd Rajput Inf., attd. 102nd Grenadiers.
Fateh Khan, Jemadar, 3rd Sappers and Miners.
Gyani Singh, Subadar, 97th Infantry.
Hari Singh, Subadar, 107th Pioneers.
Jit Singh, Jemadar, 97th Infantry.
Kanhaiya, Subadar, 97th Infantry.
Muhammad Ayub Ali Khan, Subadar, 97th Infantry.
Parbat Chand, Subadar Major, 59th Rifles.
Ram Sarup Singh, Subadar, 97th Infantry.
Rup Sing Khandka, Subadar, 2nd, attd. 1st/9th Gurkhas.
Sayad Shams-ud-din, Jemadar, 116th Mahrattas, attd. 102nd Grenadiers.
Officially reported Missing, now unofficially reported Prisoner of War.
Flynn, Sec. Lt. G. E. C., I. A. Res. of Off., attd. 103rd Mahrattas.

ADEN.

WOUNDED.
Piggford, Sec. Lt. H. G., I. A. Res. of Off., attd. 69th Punjabis.

INDIA.

ACCIDENTALLY DROWNED.

our lips, and Mansfield (when a canister made a mess of the trench not many yards away from him) was even heard to refer to our Saviour as "murry old Jesus!" These innocuous blasphemings of the holy name were a peculiar feature of the War, in which the principles of Christianity were either obliterated or falsified for the convenience of all who were engaged in it. Up in the trenches every man bore his own burden; the Sabbath was not made for man; and if a man laid down his life for his friends it was no part of his military duties. To kill an enemy was an effective action; to bring in one of our own wounded was praiseworthy, but unrelated to our war-aims. The Brigade chaplain did not exhort us to love our enemies. He was content to lead off with the hymn "How sweet the name of Jesus sounds"!

I mention this war-time dilemma of the Churches because my own mind was in rather a muddle at that time. I went up to the trenches with the intention of trying to kill someone. It was my idea of getting a bit of my own back. I did not say anything about it to anyone; but it was this feeling which took me out patrolling the mine-craters whenever an opportunity offered itself. It was a phase in my war experience—no more irrational than the rest of the proceedings, I suppose; it was an outburst of blind bravado which now seems paltry when I compare it with the behaviour of an officer like Julian Durley, who did everything that was asked of him as a matter of course.

ENEMIES

He stood alone in some queer sunless place
Where Armageddon ends. Perhaps he longed
For days he might have lived; but his young face
Gazed forth untroubled; and suddenly there thronged
Round him the hulking Germans that I shot
When for his death my brooding rage was hot.

He stared at them, half-wondering; and then
They told him how I'd killed them for his sake—
Those patient, stupid, sullen ghosts of men;
And still there seemed no answer he could make.
At last he turned and smiled. One took his hand
Because his face could make them understand.

The mail that evening had brought me a parcel from Aunt Evelyn, which contained two pots of specially good jam. Ration jam was usually in tins, and of tins it tasted. Barton gazed affectionately at the coloured label, which represented a cherry-growing landscape.

57

The label was a talisman which carried his mind safely to the home counties of England. He spoke of railway travelling. "Do you remember the five-thirty from Paddington? What a dear old train it was!" Helping himself to a spoonful of cherry jam he mentally passed through Maidenhead in a Pullman carriage. . . . The mail had also brought me the balance sheet of the Ringwell Hunt. These Hunt accounts made me feel homesick. And it appeared that the late Mr. S. Colwood had subscribed ten pounds. He must have sent it early in September, just before he was killed. No doubt he wrote the cheque in a day dream about hunting. . . .

In the meantime we were down in that frowsty smelling dug-out, listening to the cautious nibbling of rats behind the wooden walls; and above ground there was the muffled boom of something bursting. And two more officers had been killed. Not in our company though. The Germans had put up another mine that afternoon without doing us any damage. Their trenches were only a hundred and fifty yards from ours; in some places less than fifty. It was a sector of the line which specialized in mines; more than half of our 750-yard frontage was pitted with mine-craters, some of them fifty feet deep. . . .

"They were digging in front of the Bois Français Trench again last night," I remarked.

Barton had just received a message from battalion headquarters saying that the company front was to be thoroughly patrolled.

"I'll take O'Brien out with me to-night," I added.

Barton's ruddy face had resumed the worried expression which it wore when messages came from Kinjack or the Adjutant.

"All right, Kangar; but do be careful. It puts the fear of God into me when you're out there and I'm waiting for you to come in."

It put the fear of God into me too, but it was the only escape into freedom which I could contrive, up in those trenches opposite Fricourt and Mametz. And I was angry with the War.

BY 1915 THE NOTORIOUS TRENCH *system of the Western Front was well in place, running for 400 miles through Belgium and France, from the North Sea coast to the Swiss border. The trenches of the Allies and the Central Powers faced each other anywhere from a hundred yards to a mile or so apart, each defended from attack by belts of barbed wire.*

On each side, ideally, the system consisted of three lines of trenches some six to eight feet deep: the front line facing the enemy; the support line; and the reserve line (each at an interval of a hundred yards or so). These lines were connected by communication trenches up which ammunition, rations, and water were carried, and down which the wounded and dead were removed. From the front-line trench, "saps"—tenuous excavations ending in pits or shell holes—extended out into No Man's Land, to be occupied primarily at night. In the sides and bottoms of the trenches were dugouts (command-posts and dormitories for officers, who stretched out on chicken-wire bunks) and funk holes (places where the troops could sleep or cower from artillery fire). The walls of the trenches, constantly eroding, were supported by frames of wattles or wire mesh, or by corrugated iron. To avoid enfilade, the trenches were dug in a zig-zag pattern: thus walking along, every few yards one would have to turn around a traverse or bay. The side nearest the enemy was equipped with an elevated firestep, on which, every morning, the alerted troops "stood-to," peering across No Man's Land in the dawn, ready to repel an attack. As David Jones notes in In Parenthesis: "Shortly before daybreak all troops in the line stood in their appointed places, their rifles in their hands, or immediately convenient, with bayonets fixed, ready for any dawn action on the part of the enemy. When it was fully day and the dangerous half-light past, the order would come to 'stand-down and clean rifles.' This procedure was strict and binding anywhere in the forward zone, under any circumstances whatever. The same routine was observed at dusk. So that that hour occurring twice in the twenty-four, of 'stand-to,' was one of peculiar significance and there was attaching to it a degree of solemnity, in that one was conscious that from the sea dunes to the mountains, everywhere, on the whole front the two opposing lines stood alertly, waiting any eventuality." When the light came up full, if you wanted to look out into No Man's Land you used a trench periscope.

Where the trenches were not too far apart, the enemy would try to dig a tunnel or mine underneath yours and pack it with explosive, blowing you up that way. You listened to bumps and scrapes underground to catch him at it. But his usual way of harassing you was with artillery and machine-gun fire at all hours and especially at night, when you were likely to be repairing the trench parapet or the wire in the open.

By spring of 1916, when Sassoon first experienced the trenches, life there had settled into something of a routine. When in the line his battalion customarily spent two days in the front-line trench, two in the support-line, two in the reserve, and then four back at rest, which seldom meant "rest" but rather marching, polishing, cleaning, exercising, drilling, reporting, planning, and saluting. Then up to the front line again.

DOWN IN THE RESERVE line I was sitting in the gloom of the steel hut (like being inside a boiler) reading a novel by candle-light while Barton and Mansfield snored on their beds and my servant Flook sang "Dixieland" in some adjoining cubbyhole. Being in reserve was a sluggish business; in the front line we were much less morose. Outside there was a remote rumble going on, like heavy furniture being moved about in a room overhead. . . . Then the patter of rain began, and I shivered and turned chilly and thought of home and safety. It was time to be going up with that working-party. We should be out from eight till midnight, piling sandbags on the parapet of the front-line trench, which had suffered from the wet weather.

It was a pitch dark night. As we were going up across the open to the support line, the bombardment, about two miles away in the low country on our left, reached a climax. The sky winked and flick-ered like a thunderstorm gone crazy. It was a battle seen in miniature against a screen of blackness. Rocket-lights, red and white, curved up-ward; in the rapid glare of bursting explosives the floating smoke showed rufous and tormented; it was like the last hour of Gomorrah; one couldn't imagine anything left alive there. But it was only a small local attack—probably a raid by fifty men, which would be reported in two lines of the G.H.Q. communiqué. It would soon be our turn to do a raid. The Brigadier had made it quite clear that he "wanted a prisoner." One would be enough. He wanted to make certain what troops were in front of us.

Spring arrived late that year. Or was it possible that spring kept away from the front line as long as possible? Up there it seemed as though winter would last forever. On wet days the trees a mile away were like ash-grey smoke rising from the naked ridges, and it felt very much as if we were at the end of the world. And so we were; for that enemy world (which by daylight we saw through loopholes or from a hidden observation post) had no relation to the landscape of life. It had meant the end of the world for the man whose helmet was still lying about the trench with a jagged hole through it. Steel hats (which our Division had begun to wear in February) couldn't keep out a rifle bullet. . . .

By five o'clock on a frosty white morning it would be daylight. Trees and broken roofs emerged here and there from the folds of mist that drifted in a dense blur; above them were the white shoals and chasms of the sky flushed with the faint pink of dawn. Standing-to at dawn was a desolate affair. The men stamped their feet and rats scurried along the crannied parapets. But we'd had our tot of rum, and we were to be relieved that afternoon. . . . Dandelions had begun to flower along the edges of the communication trenches. This was a sign of spring, I thought, as we filed down Canterbury Avenue, with the men making jokes about the estaminet in Morlancourt. Estaminet! What a memory-evoking word! . . . It was little enough that they had to go back to.

As for me, I had more or less made up my mind to die; the idea made things easier. In the circumstances there didn't seem anything else to be done. I only mention the fact because it seems, now, so strange that I should have felt like that when I had so much of my life to lose. Strange, too, was the thought of summer. It meant less mud, perhaps, but more dust; and the "big push" was always waiting for us.

61

Safe in Morlancourt, I slept like a log. Sleep was a wonderful thing when one came back from the Line; but to wake was to remember. Talking to Joe Dottrell did me good. A new transport officer had arrived—a Remount man from England. It was said that he had been combed out of a cushy job. I was glad I'd given up the transport. Glad, too, to be able to ride out on the black mare.

After the ugly weather in the trenches a fine afternoon in the wood above Méaulte was something to be thankful for. The undergrowth had been cut down, and there were bluebells and cowslips and anemones, and here and there a wild-cherry tree in blossom. Teams of horses, harrowing the uplands, moved like a procession, their crests blown by the wind. But the rural spirit of the neighbourhood had been chased away by supply sheds and R.E. stores and the sound of artillery on the horizon. Albert (where Jules Verne used to live), with its two or three chimney-stacks and the damaged tower of the basilica, showed above a line of tall trees along the riverside; a peaceful medley of roofs as I watched it, but in reality a ruined and deserted town.

From one "bay" to another I went, stopping for a word in an undertone with the sentries; patient in their waterproof sheets they stood on the firestep, peering above the parapet until bleak daylight began to show itself. The trench was falling in badly in places after the rain. . . .

Back in the main trench, I stood on the firestep to watch the sky whitening. Sad and stricken the country emerged. . . . Down in the craters the dead water took a dull gleam from the sky. . . . and there seemed no sort of comfort left in life. My steel hat was heavy on my head while I thought how I'd been on leave last month. I remembered how I'd leant my elbows on Aunt Evelyn's front gate. (It was my last evening.) That twilight, with its thawing snow, made a comfortable picture now. John Homeward had come past with his van, plodding beside his weary horse. . . . He had pulled up for a few minutes, and we'd talked about Dixon, who had been such an old friend of his. "Ay; Tom was a good chap; I've never known a better. . . ." He had said good-bye and good-night and set his horse going again. As he turned the corner the past had seemed to go with him. . . .

And here I was, with my knobkerrie in my hand, staring across at the enemy I'd never seen. Somewhere out of sight beyond the splintered tree-tops of Hidden Wood a bird had begun to sing. Without

knowing why, I remembered that it was Easter Sunday. Standing in that dismal ditch, I could find no consolation in the thought that Christ was risen. I sploshed back to the dug-out to call the others up for "stand-to."

We came back to Morlancourt after Easter, and on the same evening a message from the Orderly Room instructed me to proceed to the Fourth Army School next morning for a month's refresher-course. Perhaps Colonel Kinjack had heard that I'd been looking for trouble. Anyhow, my personal grievance against the Germans was interrupted for at least four weeks, and a motor-bus carried me away from all possibility of dying a murky death in the mine-craters.

The star turn in the schoolroom was a massive sandy-haired High-land Major whose subject was "The Spirit of the Bayonet." Though at that time undecorated, he was afterwards awarded the D.S.O. for lecturing. He took as his text a few leading points from *The Manual of Bayonet Training.*

> To attack with the bayonet effectively requires Good Direc-tion, Strength and Quickness, during a state of wild excitement and probably physical exhaustion. The bayonet is essentially an offensive weapon. In a bayonet assault all ranks go forward to kill or be killed, and only those who have developed skill and strength by constant training will be able to kill. The spirit of the bayonet must be inculcated into all ranks, so that they go forward with that aggressive determination and confidence of superiority born of continual practice, without which a bayonet assault will not be effective.

He spoke with homicidal eloquence, keeping the game alive with genial and well-judged jokes. He had a Sergeant to assist him. The Sergeant, a tall sinewy machine, had been trained to such a pitch of frightfulness that at a moment's warning he could divest himself of all semblance of humanity. With rifle and bayonet he illustrated the Major's ferocious aphorisms, including facial expression. When told

66

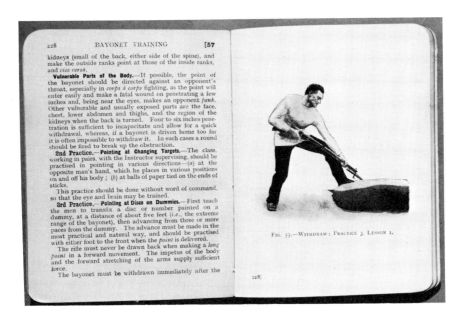

to "put on the killing face," he did so, combining it with an ultra-vindictive attitude. "To instil fear into the opponent" was one of the Major's main maxims. Man, it seemed, had been created to jab the life out of Germans. To hear the Major talk, one might have thought that he did it himself every day before breakfast. His final words were: "Remember that every Boche you fellows kill is a point scored to our side; every Boche you kill brings victory one minute nearer and shortens the war by one minute. Kill them! Kill them! There's only one good Boche, and that's a dead one!"

MAJOR (LATER COLONEL) CAMPBELL's emotional lecture-demonstration on the Spirit of the Bayonet was famous, so notable for ferocity that almost every memoirist of the war comments ironically on it. Graves argues in Good-Bye to All That that Sassoon's "The Kiss" was written "straight," as an enthusiastic endorsement of Major Campbell's points, and that only later, when his ardor for destruction was wearing off, did Siegfried present it as an ironical satire on bloodthirstiness. Late in life Sassoon told a critic planning a book about his work: "I am tired of telling people that The Kiss was intended as a satire on bayonet fighting, which I loathed—Graves's

67

statement is one of his many inaccuracies. Campbell's lecture was an abso-
lute horror. Surely I indicated in The [Memoirs of an] Infantry Officer
that I was shocked by it. Can you do something to correct this?"

But as Graves says of the poem, "It certainly comes off, whichever
way you read it."

THE KISS

To these I turn, in these I trust—
Brother Lead and Sister Steel.
To his blind power I make appeal,
I guard her beauty clean from rust.

He spins and burns and loves the air,
And splits a skull to win my praise;
But up the nobly marching days
She glitters naked, cold and fair.

Sweet Sister, grant your soldier this:
That in good fury he may feel
The body where he sets his heel
Quail from your downward darting kiss.

I came back from the Army School at the end of a hot Saturday
afternoon. The bus turned off the bumpy main road from Corbie
and began to crawl down a steep winding lane. I looked, and there
was Morlancourt in the hollow. On the whole I considered myself
lucky to be returning to a place where I knew my way about. . . .
Distant hills and hazy valleys were dazzled with sun-rays and the
glaring beams made a fiery mist in the foreground. It was jolly fine
country, I thought. I had become quite fond of it, and the end-of-
the-world along the horizon had some obscure hold over my mind
which drew my eyes to it almost eagerly, for I could still think of
trench warfare as an adventure. The horizon was quiet just now, as
if the dragons which lived there were dozing.

· · ·

"*Wednesday, 6:15 p.m. On Crawley Ridge.* Ormond up here in the Redoubt with a few men. I relieve him while he goes down to get his dinner. Very still evening; sun rather hazy. Looking across to Fricourt; trench mortars bursting in the cemetery; dull white smoke slowly floats away over grey-green grass with buttercups and saffron weeds. Fricourt; a huddle of reddish roofs; skeleton village; church tower, almost demolished, a white patch against green of Fricourt wood (full of German batteries). North, up the hill, white seams and heapings of trenches dug in chalk. Sky full of lark songs. Sometimes you can count thirty slowly and hear no sound of a shot; then the muffled pop of a rifle or a slamming 5.9 or one of our 18-pounders. Then a burst of machine-gun fire. Westward the yellow sky with a web of filmy cloud half across the sun; the ridges with blurred outlines of trees. An aeroplane droning overhead. A thistle sprouting through the chalk on the parapet; a cockchafer sailing through the air. Down the hill, the Bray-Fricourt road, white and hard. A partridge flies away, calling. Lush grass and crops of nettles; a large black slug out for his evening walk (doing nearly a mile a month)."

Well, here I was, and my incomplete life might end any minute; for although the evening air was as quiet as a cathedral, a canister soon came over quite near enough to shatter my meditations with its unholy crash and cloud of black smoke. A rat scampered across the tin

cans and burst sandbags, and trench atmosphere reasserted itself in a smell of chloride of lime. On my way to the dug-out, to fetch my revolver and attend the twilight ceremony of stand-to and rifle inspection, I heard the voice of Flook; just round a bend of the support trench he was asking one of the company bombers if he'd seen his officer bloke go along that way. Flook was in a hurry to tell me that I was to go on leave.

• • •

When Aunt Evelyn wondered whether I'd like anyone to come to dinner on my last evening . . . , I replied that I'd rather we were alone. There were very few to ask, and, as she said, people were difficult to get hold of nowadays. So, after a dinner which included two of my favourite puddings, we made the best of a bad job by playing cribbage (a game we had been addicted to when I was at home for my school holidays) while the black Persian cat washed his face with his paw and blinked contentedly at the fire which had been lit though there was no need for it, the night being warm and still.

Next morning [Aunt Evelyn] contrived to be stoically chatty until I had seen her turn back to the house door and the village taxi was rattling me down the hill. She had sensibly refrained from coming up to London to see me off. But at Waterloo Station I was visibly reminded that going back for the Push was rather rough on one's relations, however incapable they might be of sharing the experience. There were two leave trains and I watched the people coming away after the first one had gone out. Some sauntered away with assumed unconcern; they chatted and smiled. Others hurried past me with a crucified look; I noticed a well-dressed woman biting her gloved fingers; her eyes stared fixedly; she was returning alone to a silent house on a fine Sunday afternoon.

Armed with Aunt Evelyn's membership ticket (posted back to her afterwards) I had invaded the Army and Navy Stores and procured a superb salmon, two bottles of old brandy, an automatic pistol, and two pairs of wire-cutters. . . . The salmon was now my chief concern. I was concerned about its future freshness, for I had overstayed my leave by twenty-four hours, . . . but I felt that the salmon spelt safety at Battalion Headquarters. Probably the word *smelt* also entered my apprehensive mind. The brandy claimed that it had been born in 1838, so one day more or less couldn't affect its condition, as long as I kept an eye on it (for such bottles were liable to lose themselves on a leave boat). The wire-cutters were my private contribution to the Great Offensive. I had often cursed the savage bluntness of our Company's wire-cutters, and it occurred to me, in the Army and Navy Stores, that if we were going over the top we might want to cut our own wire first, to say nothing of the German wire (although our artillery would have made holes in that, I hoped). So I bought these very civilized ones, which looked almost too good

71

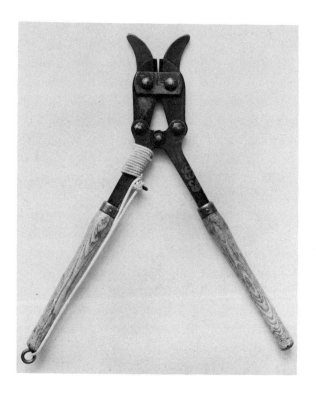

for the Front Line. The man in the Weapon Department at the Stores had been persuasive about a periscope (probably prismatic) but I came to the conclusion that a periscope was a back number in my case. I shouldn't be in the trench long enough to need it. Apart from the wire-cutters and the pistol, all other "trench requisites" appeared redundant. I couldn't see myself leading my platoon with *Mortleman's Patent Sound Absorbers* plugged in my ears, and a combined Compass-Barometer also failed to attract me.

At Havre I was instructed, by the all-knowing authority responsible for my return, to get out of the train at Corbie. Havre was a glitter of lights winking on dark slabbing water. Soon the glumly-laden train was groaning away from the wharves, and we nodded and snored through the night. Daylight came, and we crawled past green landscapes blurred with drizzling rain. Of my compartment companions

I remember nothing except that one of them talked irrepressibly about his father's farm in Suffolk. His father, he said, owned a bull who had produced sixty black and white calves. This information was received with apathy. The Battalion was at Bussy, a three-mile walk in late afternoon sunshine. I kept to the shady side of the road, for the salmon in its hamper was still my constant care. Bussy came in sight as a pleasant little place on a tributary of the Ancre. A few of our men were bathing, and I thought how young and light-hearted they looked, splashing one another and shouting. . . . How different to the trudging figures in full marching order; and how difficult to embody them in the crouching imprisonment of trench warfare!

Four British campaigns of the First World War have entered history as examples of both high heroism—or gross innocence—and flagrant staff failure: Gallipoli and Loos in 1915; the Somme in 1916; and Passchendaele in 1917. At the opening of the calamitous Battle of the Somme, Sassoon's battalion was on the front line but designated part of the reserve, through which a battalion of the Manchester Pals regiment was to pass on its way to the German positions. He thus had a grandstand seat, although not a very safe one, from which to observe the events of July 1, 1916. If he'd been in one of the attacking waves, his chances of survival would have been slim indeed: approximately three-quarters of the officers in the attacking battalions were wiped out, and half the men.

Before it took place the Battle of the Somme was referred to as the Big Push. Afterwards, it was known, at least among the survivors, as the Great Fuck-Up. General Sir Douglas Haig, persuaded by the French that the British should do something to relieve the pressure on Verdun, planned the battle for six months. Everyone hoped, and some believed, that it would end the war. Spread over an eighteen-mile front, thirteen of Haig's divisions were to attack six German divisions, opening the way for three divisions of cavalry to burst through and, flourishing lances and sabers, penetrate enemy territory to a depth of thirty miles. Preparations had been elaborate in the extreme: a whole new railway system, for example, had been built to bring up vast quantities of ammunition, supplies, and medical equipment.

The German front line was bombarded for seven days with over a million and a half shells from 1,537 guns, and the British thus forfeited surprise. The theory was that this bombardment would obliterate the German positions and the wire strung in front of them, making the infantry assault a mere walkover. Everyone believed this, including Haig, although his headquarters was fifty miles behind the front, which he'd not visited. The night before the infantry went over, he wrote in his diary: "With God's help I feel hopeful. The men are in splendid spirits. . . . The wire has never been so well cut, nor the artillery preparation so thorough." What he didn't know, but what the troops discovered on the fatal next morning, was that the artillery had done very little damage to the wire, and that the German dugouts, deeper and better constructed than anyone had imagined, had protected the bulk of the defenders from the bombardment.

At 7:30 in the morning of a beautiful day, the artillery shifted to more distant targets and 84 British battalions jumped off (43, Sassoon's among them, were in reserve behind them, and 70 more were in reserve behind them). Immediately the Germans climbed up from their battered works and dragged their machine guns to the surface. Cutting down the attackers was easy work, for the British walked upright carefully aligned, each man carrying 66 pounds of equipment. A German who witnessed the spectacle said: "The English came walking, as though they were going to the theatre or as though they were on a parade ground. We felt they were mad."

It was simply a massacre. By nightfall on July 1, almost 20,000 patriotic, guileless volunteers, the core of Kitchener's New Army, lay dead between the lines. Wounded or missing were 40,000 more. Some battalions were virtually erased, like the 10th West Yorks, of which 21 men remained out of almost 800, or the 1st Newfoundland Battalion, 91 percent destroyed. Of one 40-man platoon of the 1st Rifle Brigade, one person was left. As one commentator observed later, the opening day of the battle constituted "the greatest defeat for the British army since the Battle of Hastings." On this one day, "The British Army's loss . . . easily exceeds its battle casualties in the Crimean War, the Boer War and the Korean War combined."

The battle was costly not just in lives but in illusions too. "We were told," Sassoon remembers, "that the attack was to be on a really grand scale this time, and we believed that the results would be proportionately progressive." The day after the attack the London newspapers were proclaiming, "The Day Goes Well for Our Heroic Troops," and it was months before the whole truth leaked through the censorship. Haig doggedly kept up such pressure as he could but finally called off the campaign in the middle of November, by which time his attacking troops were still four miles this side of Bapaume, designated one of the objectives of the cavalry on the first day. Commented one man who had gone across on

July 1: "It was pure bloody murder. Douglas Haig should have been hung, drawn and quartered for what he did on the Somme. The cream of British manhood was shattered in less than six hours." Another said: "From that moment all my religion died."

NEW TRENCH, which we took over, had been a good deal knocked about, but we passed an unharassed night. We were opposite Sunken Road Trench, which was 300 yards away up a slope. Gaps had been cut in our wire for the attacking battalion to pass through. Early on the next afternoon Kinjack came up to inspect the gaps. With the assistance of his big periscope he soon discovered that the wire wasn't properly cut. It must be done that night, he said. Barton brought me the news. I was huddled up in a little dog-kennel of a dug-out, reading *Tess of the D'Urbervilles* and trying to forget about the shells which were hurrying and hurrooshing overhead. I was meditating about England, visualizing a grey day down in Sussex; dark green woodlands with pigeons circling above the tree-tops; dogs barking, cocks crowing, and all the casual tappings and twinklings of the countryside. I thought of the huntsman walking out in his long white coat with the hounds; of Parson Colwood pulling up weeds in his garden till tea-time; of Captain Huxtable helping his men get in the last load of hay while a shower of rain moved along the blurred Weald below his meadows. It was for all that, I supposed, that I was in the front-line with soaked feet, trench mouth, and feeling short of sleep, for the previous night had been vigilant though uneventful.

. . .

When I was back in the dug-out I found myself fingering with pardonable pride my . . . wire-cutters from the Army and Navy Stores. It is possible that I over-estimated their usefulness, but their presence did seem providential. Any fool could foresee what happened when troops got bunched up as they left their trench for a daylight attack; and I knew that, in spite of obstinate indentations to the source of supplies, we hadn't got a decent pair of wire-cutters in the Battalion.

The big-bugs back at Brigade and Divisional H.Q. were studying trench-maps with corrugated brows, for the "greatest battle in history" was timed to explode on Saturday morning. They were too busy to concern themselves with the ant-like activities of individual platoon commanders, and if they sent a sympathetic Staff Captain up to have a look round he couldn't produce wire-cutters like a conjuror. But the fact remained that insistence on small (and often irrelevant) details was a proverbial characteristic of Staff organization, and on the eve of battle poor old Barton would probably be filling in a "return" stating how many men in his company had got varicose veins or married their deceased wife's sister. In the meantime my casual purchase at "the Stores" had, perhaps, lessened the likelihood of the Manchesters getting bunched up and mown down by machine-guns when they went over the top to attack Sunken Road Trench. And what would the Manchesters say about the Flintshire Fusiliers if the wire wasn't properly cut? So it seemed to me that our prestige as a Regular Battalion had been entrusted to my care on a front of several hundred yards.

Anyhow, I was ready with my party as soon as it began to be dark. There were only eight of them (mostly from the other companies) and we were unable to do anything before midnight owing to rather lively shelling. I remember waiting there in the gloom and watching an unearthly little conflagration caused by some phosphorus bombs up the hill on our right. When we did get started I soon discovered that cutting tangles of barbed wire in the dark in a desperate hurry is a job that needs ingenuity, even when your wire-cutters . . . are fresh from the Army and Navy Stores. More than once we were driven in by shells which landed in front of our trench (some of them were our own dropping short); two men were wounded and some of the others were reluctant to resume work. In the first greying of dawn only three of us were still at it. Kendle (a nineteen-year-old lance-corporal from my platoon) and Worgan (one of the tough characters of our company) were slicing away for all they were worth; but as the light increased I began to realize the unimpressive effect of the snippings and the snatchings which had made such a mess of our leather gloves. We had been working three and a half hours but the hedge hadn't suffered much damage, it seemed. Kendle disappeared into the trench and sauntered back to me, puffing a surreptitious Woodbine. I was making a last onslaught on a clawing thicket which couldn't have been more hostile if it had been put there by the Ger-

mans. "We can't do any more in this daylight," said Kendle. I straightened my stiff and weary back and looked at him. His jaunty fag-smoking demeanour and freckled boyish face seemed to defy the darkness we had emerged from. That moment has impressed itself strongly on my memory; young Kendle was remarkable for his cheerfulness and courage, and his cheeky jokes. Many a company had its Kendle, until the war broke his spirit. . . . The large solicitous countenance of old man Barton now appeared above the parapet; with almost aunt-like anxiety he urged us to come in before we got sniped. But there had been no sniping that night, and the machine-gun at Wing Corner had been silent. Wing Corner was at the edge of the skeleton village of Fricourt, whose ruinous church tower was now distinctly visible against the dark green wood. The Germans, coming up from their foundering dug-outs, would soon be staring grimly across at us while they waited for the relentless bombardment to begin again. As we got down into the trench young Kendle remarked that my new wire-cutters were a fair treat.

On July the first the weather, after an early morning mist, was of the kind commonly called heavenly. Down in our frowsty cellar we breakfasted at six, unwashed and apprehensive. Our table, appropriately enough, was an empty ammunition box. At six-forty-five the final bombardment began, and there was nothing for us to do except sit round our candle until the tornado ended. For more than forty minutes the air vibrated and the earth rocked and shuddered. Through the sustained uproar the tap and rattle of machine-guns could be identified; but except for the whistle of bullets no retaliation came our way until a few 5.9 shells shook the roof of our dug-out. Barton and I sat speechless, deafened and stupefied by the seismic state of affairs, and when he lit a cigarette the match flames staggered crazily. Afterwards I asked him what he had been thinking about. His reply was "Carpet slippers and kettle-holders." My own mind had been working in much the same style, for during that cannonading cataclysm the following refrain was running in my head:

> They come as a boon and a blessing to men,
> The Something, the Owl, and the Waverley Pen.

For the life of me I couldn't remember what the first one was called. Was it the Shakespeare? Was it the Dickens? Anyhow it was an advertisement which I'd often seen in smoky railway stations. Then the bombardment lifted and lessened, our vertigo abated, and we looked at one another in dazed relief. Two Brigades of our Divi-

79

sion were now going over the top on our right. Our Brigade was to attack "when the main assault had reached its final objective." In our fortunate role of privileged spectators Barton and I went up the stairs to see what we could from Kingston Road Trench. We left Jenkins crouching in a corner, where he remained most of the day. His haggard blinking face haunts my memory. He was an example of the paralysing effect which such an experience could produce on a nervous system sensitive to noise, for he was a good officer both before and afterwards. I felt no sympathy for him at the time, but I do now. From the support-trench, which Barton called "our opera box," I observed as much of the battle as the formation of the country allowed, the rising ground on the right making it impossible to see anything of the attack towards Mametz. A small shiny black notebook contains my pencilled particulars, and nothing will be gained by embroidering them with afterthoughts. I cannot turn my field glasses on to the past.

7.45. The barrage is now working to the right of Fricourt and beyond. I can see the 21st Division advancing about three-quarters of a mile away on the left and a few Germans coming to meet them, apparently surrendering. Our men in small parties (not extended in line) go steadily on to the German front-line. Brilliant sunshine and a haze of smoke drifting along the landscape. Some Yorkshires a lit-

tle way below on the left, watching the show and cheering as if at a football match. The noise almost as bad as ever.

9.30. Came back to the dug-out and had a shave. 21st Division still going across the open, apparently without casualties. The sunlight flashes on bayonets as the tiny figures move quietly forward and disappear beyond mounds of trench débris. A few runners come back and ammunition parties go across. Trench-mortars are knocking hell out of Sunken Road Trench and the ground where the Manchesters will attack soon. Noise not so bad now and very little retaliation.

9.50. Fricourt half-hidden by clouds of drifting smoke, blue, pinkish and grey. Shrapnel bursting in small bluish-white puffs with tiny flashes. The birds seem bewildered; a lark begins to go up and then flies feebly along, thinking better of it. Others flutter above the trench with querulous cries, weak on the wing. I can see seven of our balloons, on the right. On the left our men still filing across in twenties and thirties. Another huge explosion in Fricourt and a cloud of brown-pink smoke. Some bursts are yellowish.

10.5. I can see the Manchesters down in New Trench, getting ready to go over. Figures filing down the trench. Two of them have gone out to look at our wire gaps! Have just eaten my last orange. . . . I am staring at a sunlit picture of Hell, and still the breeze shakes the yellow weeds, and the poppies glow under Crawley Ridge where some shells fell a few minutes ago. Manchesters are sending forward some scouts. A bayonet glitters. A runner comes back across the open to their Battalion Headquarters close here on the right. 21st Division still trotting along the skyline toward La Boisselle. Barrage going strong to the right of Contalmaison Ridge. Heavy shelling toward Mametz.

12.15. Quieter the last two hours. Manchesters still waiting. Germans putting over a few shrapnel shells. Silly if I got hit! Weather cloudless and hot. A lark singing confidently overhead.

1.30. Manchesters attack at 2.30. Mametz and Montauban reported taken. Mametz consolidated.

2.30. Manchesters left New Trench and apparently took Sunken Road Trench, bearing rather to the right. Could see about 400. Many walked casually across with sloped arms. There were about forty casualties on the left (from machine-guns in Fricourt). Through my glasses I could see one man moving his left arm up and down as he lay on his side; his face was a crimson patch. Others lay still in the sunlight while the swarm of figures disappeared over the hill. Fricourt was a cloud of pinkish smoke. Lively machine-gun fire on the far side of the hill. At 2.50 no one to be seen in no-man's-land except the casualties (about half-way across). Our dug-out shelled again since 2.30.

5.0. I saw about thirty of our A Company crawl across to Sunken Road from New Trench. Germans put a few big shells on the Cemetery and traversed Kingston Road with machine-gun. Manchester wounded still out there. Remainder of A Company went across—about 100 altogether. Manchesters reported held up in Bois Français Support. Their Colonel went across and was killed.

8.0. Staff Captain of our Brigade has been along. Told Barton that Seventh Division has reached its objectives with some difficulty, except on this Brigade front. Manchesters are in trouble, and Fricourt attack has failed. Several hundred prisoners brought in on our sector.

9.30. Our A Company holds Rectangle and Sunken Road. Jenkins gone off in charge of a carrying-party. Seemed all right again. C Company now reduced to six runners, two stretcher-bearers, Company Sergeant-Major, signallers, and Barton's servant. Flook away on carrying-party. Sky cloudy westward. Red sunset. Heavy gun-fire on the left.

2.30. (Next afternoon.) Adjutant has just been up here, excited, optimistic, and unshaven. He went across last night to ginger up A Company who did very well, thanks to the bombers. About 40 casu-

alties; only 4 killed. Fricourt and Rose Trench occupied this morning without resistance. I am now lying out in front of our trench in the long grass, basking in sunshine where yesterday there were bullets. Our new front-line on the hill is being shelled. Fricourt is full of troops wandering about in search of souvenirs. The village was a ruin and is now a dust heap. A gunner (Forward Observation Officer) has just been along here with a German helmet in his hand. Said Fricourt is full of dead; he saw one officer lying across a smashed machine-gun with his head bashed in—"a fine looking chap," he said, with some emotion, which rather surprised me.

8.15. Queer feeling, seeing people moving about freely between here and Fricourt. Dumps being made. Shacks and shelters being put up under skeleton trees and all sorts of transport arriving at Cemetery Cross Roads. We stay here till to-morrow morning. Feel a bit of a fraud.

At 2 a.m. we really began to move, passing through Mametz and along a communication trench. There were some badly mangled bodies about. Although I'd been with the Battalion nearly eight months, these were the first newly dead Germans I had seen. It gave me a bit of a shock when I saw, in the glimmer of daybreak, a dumpy, baggy-trousered man lying half sideways with one elbow up as if defending his lolling head; the face was grey and waxen, with a stiff little moustache; he looked like a ghastly doll, grotesque and undignified. Beside him was a scorched and mutilated figure whose contorted attitude revealed bristly cheeks, a grinning blood-smeared mouth and clenched teeth. These dead were unlike our own; perhaps it was the strange uniform, perhaps their look of butchered hostility. Anyhow they were one with the little trench direction boards whose unfamiliar lettering seemed to epitomize that queer feeling I used to have when I stared across no-man's-land, ignorant of the humanity which was on the other side.

GRAVES'S REMARKS ABOUT Sassoon's achievements at Mametz Wood indicate the modesty of Sassoon's own account.

"At 4 a.m. on July 15, we took the Méaulte-Fricourt-Bazentin road, which ran through 'Happy Valley,' and found ourselves in the more recent battle area. Wounded and prisoners came streaming past in the half light. The number of dead horses and mules shocked me; human corpses were all very well, but it seemed wrong for animals to be dragged into the war like this. . . . Just beyond Fricourt a German shell-barrage made the road impassable; so we left it and moved forward over thickly shell-pitted ground until 8 a.m., when we found ourselves on the fringe of Mametz Wood, among the dead of our own New Army Battalions who had helped to capture it. . . .

"I wondered what had happened to Siegfried and my friends of 'A' Company. We found the Battalion quite close in bivouacs; Siegfried was still alive, so were Edmund Dadd and two other 'A' Company officers. The Battalion had seen heavy fighting. . . . [At] 'The Quadrangle,' a small copse this side of Mametz Wood, . . . Siegfried distinguished himself by taking, single-handed, a battalion frontage which the Royal Irish Regiment had failed to take the day before. He went over with bombs in daylight, under covering fire from a couple of rifles, and scared away the occupants. A pointless feat, since instead of signalling for reinforcements, he sat down in the German trench and began reading a book of poems which he had brought with him. When he finally went back he did not even report. Colonel Stockwell, then in command, raged at him. The attack on Mametz Wood had been delayed for two hours because British

84

patrols were still reported to be out. 'British patrols' were Siegfried and his book of poems. 'I'd have got you a D.S.O. if only you'd shown more sense,' stormed Stockwell. Siegfried had been doing heroic things ever since I left the Battalion."

MAMETZ WOOD . . . was a dense wood of old trees and undergrowth. The Staff of our Division had assumed that the near side was now unoccupied. But as soon as we had halted in a sunken road an uproar broke out at the edge of the wood, which demonstrated with machine-guns and bombs that the Staff had guessed wrong.

Kinjack promptly ordered A Company forward to get in touch with the Royal Irish, whose covering parties were having a bombing fight in the Wood. Our men were fired on as they went along the road and forced to take cover in a quarry. I remember feeling nervous and incompetent while I wondered what on earth I should do if called on to lead a party out "into the blue." But the clouds were now reddening, and we were fed up with the whole performance. Messages

went back and our guns chucked a lot of shrapnel which burst over the near side of the Wood and enabled the Irish to withdraw. We then, as Kinjack described it afterwards, "did a guy"; but it was a slow one for we weren't back at our camping ground until 8:30 a.m. The expedition had lasted nearly eleven hours and we had walked less than three miles, which was about all we could congratulate ourselves on. The Royal Irish had had sixty casualties; we had one killed and four wounded. From a military point of view the operations had enabled the Staff to discover that Mametz Wood was still full of Germans, so that it was impossible to dig a trench on the bluff within fifty yards of it, as had been suggested. It was obvious now that a few strong patrols could have clarified the situation more economically than 1,000 men with picks and shovels. The necessary information had been obtained, however, and the Staff could hardly be expected to go up and investigate such enigmas for themselves. But this sort of warfare was a new experience for all of us, and the difficulties of extempore organization must have been considerable.

During the morning we were a silent battalion, except for snoring. Some eight-inch guns were firing about 200 yards from the hollow, but our slumbers were inured to noises which would have kept us wide awake in civilian life. We were lucky to be dry, for the sky was overcast. At one o'clock our old enemy the rain arrived in full force. Four hours' deluge left the troops drenched and disconsolate, and then Dottrell made one of his providential appearances with the rations. Dixies of hot tea, and the rum issue, made all the difference to our outlook. It seemed to me that the Quartermaster symbolized that region of temporary security which awaited us when our present adversities were ended. He had a cheery word for everyone, and his jocularity was judicious. What were the jokes he made, I wonder? Their helpfulness must be taken for granted. I can only remember his chaffing an officer named Woolman, whose dumpy figure had bulged abnormally since we came up to the battle area. Woolman's young lady in England had sent him a bullet-proof waistcoat; so far it had only caused its wearer to perspire profusely; and although reputed to be extremely vulnerable, it had inspired a humorist in his company to refer to him as "Asbestos Bill."

THE
DAYFIELD
BODY SHIELD
again
SAVES LIFE

21/-   52/6

Patent No. 5196

> Strawberry Farm, Bisley, Surrey.
> "I write to ask you to send a Double Shield, for which I enclose a cheque. It may interest you to know that the shield you sent in October last year to Sergeant Pollard was the means of saving his life. He writes to say in his letter dated 29th ulto.; 'Did I mention that the shield you sent me saved my life? When I return you shall see the dent the bullet made.'"

SIR HIRAM MAXIM says : Fully 25 per cent. of the casualties we have met so far would have been prevented by the use of this shield.

The Dayfield Body Shield

is tested, absolutely fulfilling every claim made for it. Proof against bayonet, sword and lance; also against spent bullets, shrapnel, shell splinters and grenades, Worn under the tunic, light in weight (36ozs.), comfortable in wear, and in no way impedes action. Size 17ins. by 12ins. Covered with Khaki drill. Although quite flexible, these shields thoroughly protect the vital parts, being made of specially prepared tough metal in four sections, with the points covered by steel strips which prevent penetration at these points.

Supplied to Generals, Officers of all ranks, N.C.O.'s and Men.

The Double Shield consists of two Single Shields protecting back and front, joined together by straps with curved metal plates to fit and protect the shoulders.

SINGLE SHIELD, *Post paid*, British Isles. 21/6
DOUBLE SHIELD, *Post paid*, British Isles, 53/6
If sent to the Front, 1/- extra single, 1/6 double.

Write for Illustrated Pamphlet and Testimonials.
Of Military Outfitters and Stores or direct from

Whitfield Manufacturing Co., Ld.

(Agents for the Corrugated Steel Helmets),
Vernon House, Sicilian Avenue, Southampton Row. W.C.
Where Models and Testimonials can be seen.

Fernby said that we were being sniped from the trees on both sides. Mametz Wood was a menacing wall of gloom, and now an outburst of rapid thudding explosions began from that direction. There was a sap from the Quadrangle to the Wood, and along this the Germans were bombing. In all this confusion I formed the obvious notion that we ought to be deepening the trench. Daylight would be on us at once, and we were along a slope exposed to enfilade fire from the Wood. I told Fernby to make the men dig for all they were worth, and went to the right with Kendle. The Germans had left a lot of shovels, but we were making no use of them. Two tough-looking privates were disputing the ownership of a pair of field-glasses, so I pulled out my pistol and urged them, with ferocious objurgations, to chuck all that fooling and dig. I seemed to be getting pretty handy with my pistol, I thought, for the conditions in Quadrangle Trench were giving me a sort of angry impetus. In some places it was only a foot deep, and already men were lying wounded and killed by sniping. There were high-booted German bodies, too, and in the blear beginning of daylight they seemed as much the victims of a catastrophe as the men who had attacked them. As I stepped over one of the Germans an impulse made me lift him up from the miserable ditch. Propped against the bank, his blond face was undisfigured, except by the mud which I wiped from his eyes and mouth with my coat sleeve. . . . He didn't look to be more than eighteen. Hoisting him a little higher, I thought what a gentle face he had, and remembered that this was the first time I'd ever touched one of our enemies with my hands. Perhaps I had some dim sense of the futility which had put an end to this good-looking youth. Anyhow I hadn't expected the Battle of the Somme to be quite like this.

GRAVES RECALLS HIS FIRST MEETING with Sassoon, back in November, 1915, when he was assigned to 'A' Company, Royal Welch Fusiliers, in France. Sassoon was in 'C' Company.

"A day or two after I arrived I went to visit 'C' Company Mess, where I got a friendly welcome. I noticed The Essays of Lionel Johnson lying on the table. It was the first book I had seen in France (except my own copies of Keats and Blake) that was neither a military text-book nor a rubbishy novel. I stole a look at the fly-leaf, and the name was Siegfried Sassoon. Then I looked around to find who could possibly be called Siegfried Sassoon and bring Lionel Johnson with him to the First Battalion. The answer being obvious, I got into conversation with him, and a few minutes later we set out for Béthune, being off duty until dusk, and talked about poetry.

"Siegfried Sassoon had, at that time, published only a few privately-printed pastoral pieces of eighteen-ninetyish flavour, and a satire on Masefield which, half-way through, had forgotten to be a satire and turned into rather good Masefield. We went to the cake-shop and ate cream buns. At this time I was getting my first book of poems, Over the Brazier, ready for the press; I had one or two drafts in my pocket-book and showed them to Siegfried. He frowned and said that the war should not be written about in such a realistic way. In return, he showed me some of his own poems. One of them began:

> Return to greet me, colours that were my joy,
> Not in the woeful crimson of men slain . . . .

Siegfried had not yet been in the trenches. I told him, in my old-soldier manner, that he would soon change his style."

RETURNING FROM an after dinner stroll I found that several Second Battalion officers had come to visit us. It was almost dark; these officers were standing outside our tent with Durley and the others,

and it sounded as if they were keeping up their courage with the volubility usual among soldiers who knew that they would soon be in an
attack. Among them, big and impulsive, was David Cromlech, who
had been with our Battalion for three months of the previous winter.
As I approached the group I recognized his voice with a shock of delighted surprise. He and I had never been in the same Company, but
we were close friends, although somehow or other I have hitherto left
him out of my story. On this occasion his face was only dimly dis-
cernible, so I will not describe it, though it was a remarkable one. An
instinct for aloofness which is part of my character caused me to remain in the background for a minute or two, and I now overheard
his desperately cheerful ejaculations with that infinite pang of affection often felt by a detached observer of such spontaneous behaviour.
When I joined the group we had so much to tell one another that I
very soon went back with him to his tentless hillside. On the way I
gave him a breathless account of my adventures up at Mametz Wood,

but neither of us really wanted to talk about the Somme Battle. We should probably get more than enough of it before we'd finished. He had only just joined the Second Battalion, and I was eager to hear about England. The men of his platoon were lying down a little way off; but soon their recumbent mutterings had ceased, and all around us in the gloom were sleeping soldiers and the pyramids of piled rifles. We knew that this might be our last meeting, and gradually an ultimate strangeness and simplicity overshadowed and contained our low-voiced colloquies. We talked of the wonderful things we'd do after the war; for to me David had often seemed to belong less to my war experience than to the freedom which would come after it. He had dropped his defensive exuberance now, and I felt that he was rather luckless and lonely—too young to be killed up on Bazentin Ridge. It was midnight when I left him. First thing in the morning I hurried up the hill in hope of seeing him again. Scarcely a trace remained of the battalion which had bivouacked there, and I couldn't so much as identify the spot where we'd sat on his ground sheet, until I discovered a scrap of silver paper which might possibly have belonged to the packet of chocolate we had munched while he was telling me about the month's holiday he'd had in Wales after he came out of hospital.

. . .

The reserve Echelon was an arid and irksome place to be loafing about in. Time hung heavy on our hands and we spent a lot of it lying in the tent on our outspread valises. During the sluggish midafternoon of the same Saturday I was thus occupied in economizing my energies. Durley had nicknamed our party "the eight little nigger boys," and there were now only seven of us. Most of them were feeling more talkative than I was, and it happened that I emerged from a snooze to hear them discussing "that queer bird Cromlech." Their comments reminded me, not for the first time, of the diversified impressions which David made on his fellow Fusiliers.

At his best I'd always found him an ideal companion, although his opinions were often disconcerting. But no one was worse than he was at hitting it off with officers who distrusted cleverness and disliked unreserved utterances. In fact he was a positive expert at putting people's backs up unintentionally. He was with our Second Battalion for a few months before they transferred him to "the First," and during that period the Colonel was heard to remark that young Cromlech threw his tongue a hell of a lot too much, and that it was about time he gave up reading Shakespeare and took to using soap and water. He had, however, added, "I'm agreeably surprised to find that he isn't windy in trenches."

David certainly was deplorably untidy, and his absent-mindedness when off duty was another propensity which made him unpopular. Also, as I have already hinted, he wasn't good at being "seen but not heard." "Far too fond of butting in with his opinion before he's been asked for it," was often his only reward for an intelligent suggestion. Even Birdie Mansfield (who had knocked about the world too much to be intolerant) was once heard to exclaim, "Unless you watch it, my son, you'll grow up into the most bumptious young prig God ever invented!"—this protest being a result of David's assertion that all sports except boxing, football, and rock climbing were snobbish and silly.

From the floor of the tent, Holman (a spick and span boy who had been to Sandhurst and hadn't yet discovered that it was unwise to look down on temporary officers who "wouldn't have been wanted in the Regiment in peace time") was now saying, "Anyhow, I was at Clitherland with him last month, and he fairly got on people's nerves with his hot air about the Battle of Loos, and his brain-waves about who really wrote the Bible." Durley then philosophically observed, "Old Longneck certainly isn't the sort of man you meet every day. I can't always follow his theories myself, but I don't mind betting that he'll go a long way—provided he isn't pushing up daisies when Peace breaks out." Holman (who had only been with us a few days and soon became more democratic) brushed Durley's defence aside with "The blighter's never satisfied unless he's turning something upside down. I actually heard him say that Homer was a woman. Can you beat that? And if you'll believe me he had the darned sauce to give me a sort of pi-jaw about going out with girls in Liverpool. If you ask me, I think he's a rotten outsider, and the sooner he's pushing up daisies the better." Whereupon Perrin (a quiet man of thirty-five who was sitting in a corner writing to his wife) stopped the discussion by saying, "Oh, dry up, Holman! For all we know the poor devil may be dead by now."

The Division had now been in action for a week. Next day they were to be relieved. . . . I went down to the crossroads with Dottrell, and there we waited hour after hour. . . . We sat among some barley on the bank above the road, as time passed we conversed companionably, keeping ourselves awake with an occasional drop of rum from his flask. I always enjoyed being with Dottrell, and that night the husky-voiced old campaigner was more eloquent than he realized. In the simplicity of his talk there was a universal tone which seemed to be summing up all the enduring experience of an Infantry Division. For him it was a big thing for the Battalion to be coming back from a battle, though, as he said, it was a new Battalion every few months now.

An hour before dawn the road was still an empty picture of moonlight. The distant gun-fire had crashed and rumbled all night,

muffled and terrific with immense flashes, like waves of some tumult
of water rolling along the horizon. Now there came an interval of silence in which I heard a horse neigh, shrill and scared and lonely.
Then the procession of the returning troops began. The camp-fires
were burning low when the grinding jolting column lumbered back.
The field guns came first, with nodding men sitting stiffly on weary
horses, followed by wagons and limbers and field-kitchens. After this
rumble of wheels came the infantry, shambling, limping, straggling
and out of step. If anyone spoke it was only a muttered word, and the
mounted officers rode as if asleep. The men had carried their emergency water in petrol-cans, against which bayonets made a hollow
clink; except for the shuffling feet, this was the only sound. Thus,
with an almost spectral appearance, the lurching brown figures flitted
past with slung rifles and heads bent forward under basin-helmets.
Moonlight and dawn began to mingle, and I could see the barley
swaying indolently against the sky. A train groaned along the riverside, sending up a cloud of whitish fiery smoke against the gloom of
the trees. The Flintshire Fusiliers were a long time arriving. On the
hill behind us the kite balloon swayed slowly upward with straining
ropes, its looming bulbous body reflecting the first pallor of daybreak.
Then, as if answering our expectancy, a remote skirling of bagpipes
began, and the Gordon Highlanders hobbled in. But we had been

94

sitting at the crossroads nearly six hours, and faces were recognizable, when Dottrell hailed our leading Company.

Soon they had dispersed and settled down on the hillside, and were asleep in the daylight which made everything seem ordinary. None the less I had seen something that night which overawed me. It was all in the day's work—an exhausted Division returning from the Somme Offensive—but for me it was as though I had watched an army of ghosts. It was as though I had seen the War as it might be envisioned by the mind of some epic poet a hundred years hence.

On Saturday afternoon we made a short train journey and then marched four easy miles to a village called La Chaussée. Twenty-four hours' rest and a shave had worked the usual miracle with the troops (psychological recovery was a problem which no one had time to recognize as existent) and now we were away from the Line for at least a fortnight. It was a dusty golden evening, and the road led us through quiet green country. Delusively harmonious, perhaps, is that retrospective picture of the Battalion marching at ease along an unfrequented road, at the end of a July afternoon, with Colonel Kinjack riding rather absentmindedly in front, or pulling up to watch us go past him—his face thoughtful and indulgent and expressing something of the pride and satisfaction which he felt.

So it will go on, I thought; in and out, in and out, till something happens to me. We had come along the same road last January. Only five officers of that lot were with us now: not many of them had been killed, but they had "faded away" somehow or other, and my awareness of this created a deceptive sense of "the good old days." Yesterday afternoon I'd heard that Cromlech had been killed up at High Wood. This piece of news had stupefied me, but the pain hadn't begun to make itself felt yet, and there was no spare time for personal grief when the Battalion was getting ready to move back to Divisional Rest. To have thought about Cromlech would have been calamitous. "Rotten business about poor old 'Longneck,' " was the only comment that Durley, Dottrell and the others allowed themselves. And after all he wasn't the only one who'd gone west lately. It was queer how the men seemed to take their victimization for granted. In and out; in and out; singing and whistling, the column swayed in front of me, much the same length as usual, for we'd had less than a hundred casualties up at Bazentin. But it was a case of every man for himself, and the corporate effect was optimistic and untroubled. A London editor driving along the road in a Staff car would have remarked that the spirit of the troops was amazing. And so it was. But somehow the newspaper men always kept the horrifying realities of the War out of their articles, for it was unpatriotic to be bitter, and the dead were assumed to be gloriously happy. However, it was no use worrying about all that; I was part of the Battalion, and now I'd got to see about getting the men settled into billets.

Some Australians had been in the billets at La Chaussée, and (if they will pardon me for saying so) had left them in a very bad state. Sanitation had been neglected, and the inhabitants were complaining furiously that their furniture had been used for firewood. Did the Australians leave anything else behind them, I wonder? For some of them had been in Gallipoli, and it is possible that dysentery germs were part of the legacy they left us.

The fact remains that I awoke on Monday morning feeling far from well and, after a mechanical effort to go on parade in a glare of sunlight, took refuge in the cavernous bedroom which I occupied alone. Feeling worse and worse, in the evening I remembered that I

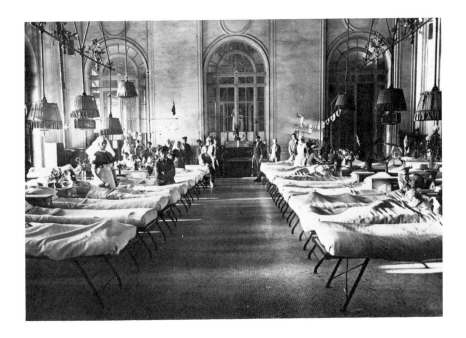

possessed a thermometer, which had been handed over to me when I was Transport Officer. I had never taken the temperatures of any of the horses, but I now experimented shakily on myself. When I saw that it indicated 105° I decided that the thing was out of order; but next morning I was confusedly aware that Flook had fetched the doctor, and by the afternoon I was unbelievably at the New Zealand Hospital, which was in a substantial old building in the middle of Amiens.

. . .

The advantages of being ill were only too obvious. Lying awake in the large lofty ward on my fourth night, I was aware that I was feeling rather run down, but much better—almost too well, in fact. That evening my temperature had been normal, which reminded me that this change from active service to invalidism was an acute psychological experience. The door to safety was half open, and though an impartial New Zealand doctor decided one's destiny, there was a not unnatural impulse to fight for one's own life instead of against the Germans. Less than two weeks ago I'd been sitting in a tent thinking noble thoughts about sharing the adversities of my fellow

Fusiliers. But that emotional defence wouldn't work now, and the unutterable words "wangle my way home" forced their way obstinately to the foreground, supported by a crowd of smug-faced excuses.

Durley and the Adjutant had visited me that afternoon; they'd joked with me about how well I was looking. While they were with me I had talked about coming back in a few days, and I'd genuinely felt as if I wanted to. But they took my fortitude away with them, and now I was foreseeing that another night's rest would make me look indecently healthy for a man in a hospital. "I suppose they'll all think I'm swinging the lead," I thought. Turning the last few months over in my mind, I argued with myself that I had done all that was expected of me. "Oh God," I prayed, "do get me sent down to the Base!" (How often was that petition whispered during the War?) To-day I had seen young Allgood's name in the Roll of Honour—a bit of news which had slammed the door on my four weeks at the Army School and provided me with a secondary sorrow, for I was already feeling sufficiently miserable about my friend Cromlech. I sympathized with myself about Allgood, for I had been fond of him. But he was only one among thousands of promising young men who had gone west since the 1st of July. Sooner or later I should probably get killed too. A breath of wind stirred the curtains, blowing them inward from the tall windows with a rustling sigh. The wind came from the direction of the Somme, and I could hear the remote thudding of the guns. Everyone in the ward seemed to be asleep except the boy whose bed had screens round it. The screens were red and a light glowed through them. Ever since he was brought in he'd been continually calling to the nurse on duty. Throughout the day this had gradually got on everyone's nerves, for the ward was already full of uncontrollable gasps and groans. Once I had caught a glimpse of his white face and miserable eyes. Whatever sort of wound he'd got he was making the most of it, had been the opinion of the man next to me (who had himself got more than he wanted, in both legs). But he must be jolly bad, I thought now, as the Sister came from behind the screen again. His voice went on, in the low, rapid, even tone of delirium. Sometimes I could catch what he said, troubled and unhappy and complaining. Someone called Dicky was on his mind, and he kept on crying out to Dicky. "Don't go out, Dicky; they snipe like hell!" And then, "Curse the Wood. . . . Dicky, you fool, don't go out!" . . . All the horror of the Somme attacks was in that raving;

all the darkness and the dreadful daylight. . . . I watched the Sister come back with a white-coated doctor; the screen glowed comfortingly; soon the disquieting voice became inaudible and I fell asleep. Next morning the screens had vanished; the bed was empty, and ready for someone else.

DIED OF WOUNDS

His wet white face and miserable eyes
Brought nurses to him more than groans and sighs:
But hoarse and low and rapid rose and fell
His troubled voice: he did the business well.

The ward grew dark; but he was still complaining
And calling out for "Dickie." "Curse the Wood!
"It's time to go. O Christ, and what's the good?
"We'll never take it, and it's always raining."

I wondered where he'd been; then heard him shout,
"They snipe like hell! O Dickie, don't go out" . . .
I fell asleep . . . Next morning he was dead;
And some Slight Wound lay smiling on the bed.

By the end of August I was back at Butley with a month's sick leave and the possibility of an extension. So for the first week or two I forget the future and enjoyed being made a fuss of by Aunt Evelyn. My outlook on the War was limited to the Battalion I had served with. After being kept out of the Line for nearly five weeks, they were expecting to be moved up at any moment.

． ． ．

I received two letters from Dottrell, written on consecutive days, but delivered by the same post. The first one began: "The old Batt. is having a rough time. We were up in the front a week ago, and lost

200 men in three days. The aid-post, a bit of a dug-out hastily made, was blown in. At the time it contained 5 wounded men, 5 stretcher-bearers, and the doctor. All were killed except the Doc. who was buried in the débris. He was so badly shaken when dug out that he had to be sent down, and will probably be in England by now. It is a hell of a place up there. The Batt. is attacking today. I hope they have better luck. The outlook is not rosy. Very glad to hear you are sitting up and taking nourishment. A lot of our best men have been knocked out recently. We shall soon want another Battn. All the boys send their love and best wishes in which your humble heartily joins."

The second letter, which I chanced to open and read first, was the worst of the two.

"Dear Kangaroo. . . . Just a line to let you know what rotten bad luck we had yesterday. We attacked Ginchy with a very weak Battn. (about 300) and captured the place but were forced out of half of it—due to the usual thing. Poor Edmunds was killed leading his Coy. Also Perrin. Durley was badly wounded, in neck and chest, I think. It is terrible to think of these two splendid chaps being cut off, but I hope Durley pulls through. Asbestos Bill died of wounds. Fernby, who was O.C. Bombers, very badly hit and not expected to live. Several others you don't know also killed. Only two officers got back without being hit. C.S.M. Miles and Danby both killed. The Battn. is *not now* over strength for rations! The rest of the Brigade suffered in proportion. Will write later. Very busy." . . .

I walked about the room, whistling and putting the pictures straight. Then the gong rang for luncheon. Aunt Evelyn drew my attention to the figs, which were the best we'd had off the old tree that autumn.

At the beginning of January David got himself passed for General Service abroad. I was completely taken by surprise when he came back and told me. Apparently the doctor asked him whether he wanted some more home service, but a sudden angry pride made him ask to be given G. S. A couple of weeks later he'd had his final leave and I was seeing him off at Liverpool Station.

A glum twenty-one-year-old veteran (unofficially in charge of a batch of young officers going out for the first time) he butted his way along the crowded platform with shoulders hunched, collar turned up to his ears, and hands plunged in pockets. A certain philosophic finality was combined with the fidgety out-of-luck look which was not unusual with him. "I've reduced my kit to a minimum this time. No revolver. I've worked it out that the chances are about five to one against my ever using it," he remarked, as he stood shuffling his feet to try and keep them warm. He hadn't explained how he'd worked the chances out, but he was always fond of a formula. Then the train began to move and he climbed awkwardly into his compartment. "Give my love to old Joe when you get to the First Battalion," was my final effort at heartiness. He nodded with a crooked smile. Going out for the third time was a rotten business and his face showed it.

"I ought to be going with him," I thought, knowing that I could have got G. S. at my last Board if I'd had the guts to ask for it. But how could one ask for it when there was a hope of getting a few more days with the Cheshire and the weather was so perishing cold out in France? "What a queer mixture he is," I thought, as I wandered absent-mindedly away from the station. Nothing could have been more cheerless than the rumbling cobbled street by the Docks, with dingy warehouses shutting out the dregs of daylight and an ash-coloured sky which foretold some more snow.

Resolving to make the most of my last day at the Base, I went down to Rouen early in the afternoon without having wasted any time in applying for leave from the Adjutant. A tram took me most of the way; the city looked fine as we crossed the river. There wasn't so very much to be done when I got there, but the first thing was to have a hair-cut. I'd had one a week ago, but this one might have to last me a longish while, for I wasn't keen on Battalion barbers. So I told the man to cut off as much as he could, and while he clipped and snipped I gazed gloomily at myself in the glass, speculating prosaically on the probabilities of my head of hair ever needing another trim up. A captain in the next chair had been through the whole repertoire—hair-cut, shave, shampoo, face-massage, and friction. "Now I feel a quid better," he remarked when he got up to go. He was wearing trench boots and was evidently on his way to the Line. I had heard him treating the barber, who spoke English, to a panegyric on the prospects of an Allied success in the Spring. "We're going to give them the knock all right this journey!" The barber asked him about a long scar which seamed his head. He smiled: "A souvenir of Devil's Wood." I wondered how much longer he would retain his enthusiasm for the Western Front. Personally I preferred rambling around Rouen and pretending that I was an ordinary peace-time tourist. In the old quarters of the town one could stroll about without meeting many English soldiers.

Later on I was going to the Hôtel de la Poste for a valedictory bath and dinner. In the meantime I was content to stare at shop-windows and explore side streets. It was a Saturday afternoon and the people were busy marketing. At the end of my wanderings I went into the Cathedral, leaving behind me the bustling Square and the sallow gusty sunset which flared above the roofs. In the Cathedral, perhaps, I could escape from the War for a while, although the Christian Religion had apparently no claim to be regarded as a Benevolent Neutral Power. . . . I remained there after the service had ended. Gradually, the glory faded from the rose-window above the organ. I looked at all the windows, until their lights were only blurs and patches, and the prophets and martyrs robed in blue and crimson and green were merged in outer darkness.

. . .

The Hôtel de la Poste hadn't altogether modernized its interior, but it contained much solid comfort and supplied the richest meals in Rouen. Consequently it was frequented by every British officer employed in the district, and had become a sort of club for those indispensable residents—so much so that strong suggestions had been advanced by senior officers to the effect that the *Poste* should be put out of bounds for all Infantry subalterns on their way to the Line. The place, they felt, was becoming too crowded, and the deportment of a "temporary gentleman" enjoying his last decent dinner was apt to be more suitable to a dug-out than a military club.

Leaning back in a wicker chair, I enjoyed the after-effects of a hot bath and wondered what I'd have for dinner. The lift came sliding down from nowhere to stop with a dull bump. A bulky grey-haired Colonel, with green tabs and a Coronation Medal, stepped heavily out, leaning on a stick and glaring around him from under a green and gold cap and aggressive eyebrows. His disapproval focused itself on a group of infantry subalterns whose ungainly legs were cumbered with high trench boots; trench-coats and haversacks were slung untidily across their chairs; to-night, or to-morrow, or "some old time or other" they'd be crawling up to the War in an over-ventilated reinforcement train, gazing enviously at the Red Cross trains which passed them—going the other way—and disparaging the French landscape, "so different to good old Blighty." Compared with "the troops," who travelled in vans designed for horses and cattle, they were in clover.

The Colonel, on the other hand, probably supervised an office full of clerks who made lists of killed, wounded, and reinforcements. I had visited such a place myself in an attempt to get my name transferred to the First Battalion, and had been received with no civility at all. They were all much too busy to rearrange the private affairs of a dissatisfied second-lieutenant, as might have been expected. But the contrast between the Front Line and the Base was an old story, and at any rate the Base Details were at a disadvantage as regards the honour and glory which made the War such an uplifting experience for those in close contact with it. I smiled sardonically at the green and gold Colonel's back view.

BASE DETAILS

If I were fierce, and bald, and short of breath,
    I'd live with scarlet Majors at the Base,
And speed glum heroes up the line to death.
    You'd see me with my puffy petulant face,
Guzzling and gulping in the best hotel,
    Reading the Roll of Honour. "Poor young chap,"
I'd say—"I used to know his father well;
    Yes, we've lost heavily in this last scrap."
And when the war is done and youth stone dead,
I'd toddle safely home and die—in bed.

The lift ascended again, leaving a confused murmur of male voices and a clatter of feet on the polished wood floor. Officers pushed through the swing-doors in twos and threes, paused to buy an English paper from the concierge, vanished to hang up their overcoats, and straddled in again, pulling down their tunics and smoothing their hair, conscious of gaiters, neatly-fitting or otherwise. Young cavalrymen were numerous, their superior social connections demonstrated by well-cut riding boots and predominantly small heads. Nice-looking young chaps with nice manners, they sipped cocktails and stood up respectfully when a Cavalry Brigadier strode past them. The Cavalry were still waiting for their chance on the Western Front. . . . Would they ever get it, I wondered. Personally, I thought it would be a pity if they did, for I disliked the idea of a lot of good horses being killed and wounded, and I had always been soft-hearted about horses. By the time I'd finished my dinner and a bottle of Burgundy, I felt soft-

"GOOD-BYE, OLD MAN"

An incident on the road to a battery position in Southern Flanders.

hearted about almost everything. The large dining-room was full of London Clubmen dressed as Colonels, Majors, and Captains with a conscientious objection to physical discomfort. But, after all, somebody had to be at the Base; modern warfare offered a niche for everyone, and many of them looked better qualified for a card-table than a military campaign. They were as much the victims of circumstances as the unfortunate troops in the trenches. Puffing a cigar, I decided that there was a tolerant view to be taken about almost everybody, especially after a good dinner at the Hôtel de la Poste.

The Second Battalion of the Flintshire Fusiliers had recently returned from two months in the Cléry sector of the Somme Front, where they had endured some of the severest weather of the War. Battalion records relate that there were no braziers in the trenches, fuel was so scarce that wooden crosses were taken from casual graves, and except for the tepid tea that came up in tins wrapped in straw,

food was mostly cold. Major-General Whincop, who commanded the Division, had made himself obnoxiously conspicuous by forbidding the Rum Ration. . . . He also thought that smoking impaired the efficiency of the troops and would have liked to restrict their consumption of cigarettes. General Whincop had likewise demonstrated his independence of mind earlier in the War by forbidding the issue of steel helmets to his Division. His conservative objection (which was based on a belief that this new War Office luxury would weaken the men's fighting spirit—"make them soft," in fact) was, of course, only a flash in the pan (or brain-pan) and Whincop's reputation as an innovator was mainly kept alive by his veto on the Rum Ration. G.O.C.s, like platoon commanders, were obliged to devise "stunts" to show their keenness, and opportunities for originality were infrequent. But since 1918 Generals have received their full share of ridicule and abuse, and it would not surprise me if someone were to start a Society for the Prevention of Cruelty to Great War Generals. If such a Society were formed, I, for one, would gladly contribute my modest half-guinea per annum; for it must be remembered that many an unsuccessful General had previously been the competent Colonel of an Infantry Battalion, thereby earning the gratitude and admiration of his men.

Anyhow, the frost had been intense, and owing to the rationing of coal in England the issue to the Army had been limited and coke-issues had caused many cases of coke-fume poisoning where the men slept in unventilated dug-outs. . . . This miserable experience . . . had ended with a thaw and a hundred cases of trench-feet. . . .

SUICIDE IN THE TRENCHES

I knew a simple soldier boy
Who grinned at life in empty joy,
Slept soundly through the lonesome dark,
And whistled early with the lark.

In winter trenches, cowed and glum,
With crumps and lice and lack of rum,
He put a bullet through his brain.
No one spoke of him again.

. . . .

You smug-faced crowds with kindling eye
Who cheer when soldier lads march by,
Sneak home and pray you'll never know
The hell where youth and laughter go.

Palm Sunday was on April 1st that year. On April 2nd we left Camp 13. No one wanted to see it again, and as we went up the hill to the Corbie road the smoke from the incinerators made the place look as if we had set fire to it.

I had a feeling that we were marching away to a better land. Camp 13 had clogged our minds, but the troops were in better spirits to-day and the Battalion seemed to have recovered its consciousness as a unit. The wind was blowing cold enough for snow, but the sun

shone and wintry weather couldn't last much longer. Where were we walking to, I wondered; for this was known to be the first stage of a longish migration northwards. Arras, perhaps; rumours of an impending battle there had been active lately. As second-in-command of the Company I went along behind it, rather at my ease. Watching the men as they plodded patiently on under their packs, I felt as if my own identity was becoming merged in the Battalion. We were on the move and the same future awaited all of us (though most of the men had bad boots and mine were quite uncomfortable).

More light-hearted than I'd been for some time, I contemplated my Company Commander, who was in undisputed occupation of a horse which looked scarcely up to his weight. Captain Leake had begun by being rude to me. I never discovered the reason.

Next day's march took us to Beauval, along a monotonous eight mile stretch of the main road from Amiens to St. Pol. . . . We passed into another "Army area"; the realm of Rawlinson was left behind us and our self-sacrificing exertions were now to be directed by

Allenby. Soon after entering the Allenby Area we sighted a group of
mounted officers who had stationed themselves under the trees by
the roadside. Word was passed back that it was the Corps Commander. Since there were only three Corps Commanders in each
Army they were seldom seen, so it was with quite a lively interest
that we put ourselves on the alert to eyes-left this one. While we
were trudging stolidly nearer to the great man, Colonel Easby detached himself from the head of the column, rode up to the General,
and saluted hopefully. The Corps Commander (who was nothing
much to look at, for his interesting accumulation of medal-ribbons
was concealed by a waterproof coat) ignored our eyes-lefting of him;
he was too busy bellowing at poor Colonel Easby, whom he wel-
comed thus. C.C. "Are you stuck to that bloody horse?" Col. E.
"No, sir." (Dismounts hastily and salutes again.) As Leake's Company went by, the General was yelling something about why the hell
hadn't the men got the muzzles of their rifles covered (this being one
of his "special ideas"). "Pity he don't keep his own muzzle covered,"
remarked someone in the ranks, thereby voicing a prevalent feeling.
The Corps Commander was equally abusive because the "Cookers"
were carrying brooms and other utilitarian objects. Also the Com-

panies were marching with fifty yard intervals between them (by a special order of the late Rawlinson). In Allenby's Army the intervals between Companies had to be considerably less, as our Colonel was now finding out. However, the episode was soon behind us and the "Cookers" rumbled peacefully on their way, brooms and all, emitting smoke and stewing away at the men's dinners.

We started from Beauval at four o'clock on a sunny afternoon and went another eight miles to a place called Lucheux. . . . There is nothing in all this, the reader will expostulate. But there was a lot in it, for us. We were moving steadily nearer to the Spring Offensive; for those who thought about it the days had an ever intensifying significance. For me, the idea of death made everything seem vivid and valuable. The War could be like that to a man, until it drove him to drink and suffocated his finer apprehensions.

Among the troops I observed a growing and almost eager expectancy; their cheerfulness increased; something was going to happen to them; perhaps they believed that the Arras Battle would end the War. It was the same spirit which had animated the Army before the Battle of the Somme. And now, once again, we could hear along the horizon that blundering doom which bludgeoned armies into material for military histories. "That way to the Sausage Machine!" some old soldier exclaimed as we passed a signpost marked *Arras, 32 k.*

On Saturday afternoon we came to Saulty, which was only ten miles from Arras and contained copious indications of the Offensive, in the form of ammunition and food dumps and the tents of a Casualty Clearing Station. A large Y.M.C.A. canteen gladdened the rank and file, and I sent my servant there to buy a pack full of Woodbines for an emergency which was a certainty. Canteens and *estaminets* would be remote fantasies when we were in the devastated area. Twelve dozen packets of Woodbines in a pale green cardboard box

were all that I could store up for the future consolation of B Company; but they were better than nothing and the box was no weight for my servant to carry.

We were at the end of a journey which had begun twelve days before, when we started from Camp 13. Stage by stage, we had marched to the life-denying region which from far away had threatened us with the blink and growl of its bombardments. Now we were groping and stumbling along a deep ditch to the place appointed for us in the zone of inhuman havoc. There must have been some hazy moonlight, for I remember the figures of men huddled against the sides of communication trenches; seeing them in some sort of ghastly glimmer (was it, perhaps, the diffused whiteness of a sinking flare beyond the ridge?) I was doubtful whether they were asleep or dead, for the attitudes of many were like death, grotesque and distorted.

But this is nothing new to write about, you will say; just a weary company, squeezing past dead or drowsing men while it sloshes and stumbles to a front-line trench. Nevertheless that night relief had its significance for me, though in human experience it had been multiplied a millionfold. I, a single human being with my little stock of earthly experience in my head, was entering once again the veritable gloom and disaster of the thing called Armageddon. And I saw it then, as I see it now—a dreadful place, a place of horror and desolation which no imagination could have invented. Also it was a place where a man of strong spirit might know himself utterly powerless against death and destruction, and yet stand up and defy gross darkness and stupefying shell-fire, discovering in himself the invincible resistance of an animal or an insect, and an endurance which he might, in after days, forget or disbelieve.

By ten o'clock I was above ground again, in charge of a fatigue party. We went half-way back to St. Martin, to an ammunition dump, whence we carried up boxes of trench mortar bombs. I carried a box myself, as the conditions were vile and it seemed the only method of

convincing the men that it had to be done. We were out nearly seven hours; it rained all day and the trenches were a morass of glue-like mud. The unmitigated misery of that carrying party was a typical infantry experience of discomfort without actual danger. Even if the ground had been dry the boxes would have been too heavy for most of the men; but we were lucky in one way; the wet weather was causing the artillery to spend an inactive Sunday. It was a yellow corpse-like day, more like November than April, and the landscape was desolate and treeless. What we were doing was quite unexceptional; millions of soldiers endured the same sort of thing and got badly shelled into the bargain. Nevertheless I can believe that my party, staggering and floundering under its loads, would have made an impressive picture of "Despair."

We were among the débris of the intense bombardment of ten days before . . . and wherever we looked the mangled effigies of the dead were our *memento mori*. Shell-twisted and dismembered, the Germans maintained the violent attitudes in which they had died.

I . . . started to explore a narrow sap on the left side of the trench. (Not that it matters whether it was on the left side or the right, but it appears to be the only detail I can remember; and when all is said and done, the War was mainly a matter of holes and ditches.) What I expected to find along that sap, I can't say. Finding nothing, I stopped to listen. There seemed to be a lull in the noise of the attack along the line. A few machine-guns tapped, spiteful and spasmodic. High up in the fresh blue sky an aeroplane droned and glinted. I thought what a queer state of things it all was, and then decided to take a peep at the surrounding country. This was a mistake which ought to have put an end to my terrestrial adventures, for no sooner had I popped my silly head out of the sap than I felt a stupendous blow in the back between my shoulders. My first notion was that a bomb had hit me from behind, but what had really happened was that I had been sniped from in front. . . . I leant against the side of the sap and shut my eyes. . . . When I reopened them Sergeant Baldock was beside me, discreet and sympathetic, and to my surprise I discovered that I wasn't dead. He helped me back to the trench, gently investigated my wound, put a field-dressing on it, and left me sitting there while he went to bring up some men.

My exodus from the Front Line was a garrulous one. A German bullet had passed through me leaving a neat hole near my right shoulder-blade and this patriotic perforation had made a different man of me. I now looked at the War, which had been a monstrous tyrant, with liberated eyes. For the time being I had regained my right to call myself a private individual.

The first stage of my return journey took me to the Advanced Dressing Station at Henin. My servant went with me, carrying my haversack. He was a quiet clumsy middle-aged man who always did his best and never complained. While we picked our way along the broken ground of Henin Hill I continued talkative, halting now and again to recover breath and take a last stare at the blighted slope where yesterday I had stumbled to and fro with my working party.

The sky was now overcast and the landscape grey and derelict. The activities of the attack had subsided, and we seemed to be walk-

ing in a waste land where dead men had been left out in the rain after being killed for no apparent purpose. Here and there, figures could be seen moving toward the Dressing Station, some of them carrying stretchers.

It was the mid-day stagnation which usually followed an early morning attack. The Dressing Station was a small underground place crowded with groaning wounded. Two doctors were doing what they could for men who had paid a heavy price for their freedom. My ego-centricity diminished among all that agony. I remember listening to an emotional padre who was painfully aware that he could do nothing except stand about and feel sympathetic. The consolations of the Church of England weren't much in demand at an Advanced Dressing Station.

I was told to go on to a place called "B. Echelon," which meant another three miles of muddy walking. Beat to the world, I reached B. Echelon, and found our Quartermaster . . . with several officers

newly arrived from the Base and one or two back from leave. Stimulated by a few gulps of whisky and water, I renewed my volubility and talked nineteen to the dozen until the kind Quartermaster put me into the mess-cart which carried me to a crossroad where I waited for a motor bus. There, after a long wait, I shook hands with my servant, and the handshake seemed to epitomize my good-bye to the Second Battalion. . . . In the bus, wedged among "walking wounded," I was aware that I had talked quite enough. For an hour and a half we bumped and swayed along ruined roads till we came to the Casualty Clearing Station at Warlencourt.

Next afternoon a train (with 500 men and 35 officers on board) conveyed me to a Base Hospital. My memories of that train are strange and rather terrible, for it carried a cargo of men in whose minds the horrors they had escaped from were still vitalized and violent. Many of us still had the caked mud of the war zone on our boots and clothes, and every bandaged man was accompanied by his battle experience. Although many of them talked lightly and even facetiously about it, there was an aggregation of enormities in the atmosphere of that train. I overheard some slightly wounded officers who were excitedly remembering their adventures up at Wancourt, where they'd been bombed out of a trench in the dark. Their jargoning voices mingled with the rumble and throb of the train as it journeyed—so safely and sedately—through the environing gloom. The Front Line was behind us; but it could lay its hand on our hearts, though its bludgeoning reality diminished with every mile. It was as if we were pursued by the Arras Battle which had now become a huge and horrible idea. We might be boastful or sagely reconstructive about our experience, in accordance with our different characters. But our minds were still out of breath and our inmost thoughts in disorderly retreat from bellowing darkness and men dying out in shell-holes under the desolation of returning daylight. We were the survivors; few among us would ever tell the truth to our friends and relations in England. We were carrying something in our heads which belonged to us alone, and to those we had left behind us in the battle. . . .

We reached our destination after midnight, and the next day I was able to write in my diary: "I am still feeling warlike and quite prepared to go back to the Battalion in a few weeks; I am told that my wound will be healed in a fortnight. The doctor here says I am a lucky man as the bullet missed my jugular vein and spine by a fraction of an inch. I know it would be better for me not to go back to England, where I should probably be landed for at least three months and then have all the hell of returning again in July or August." But in spite of my self-defensive scribble I was in London on Friday evening and by no means sorry to be carried through the crowd of patriotic spectators at Charing Cross Station. My stretcher was popped into an ambulance which took me to a big hospital at Denmark Hill. At Charing Cross a woman handed me a bunch of flowers and a leaflet by the Bishop of London who earnestly advised me to lead a clean life and attend Holy Communion.

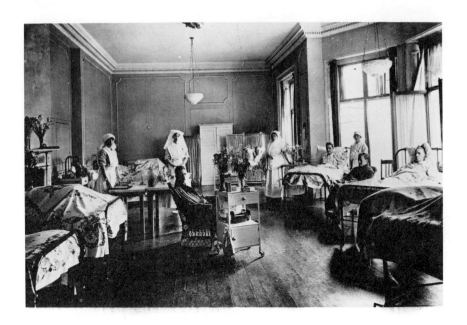

The first few days were like lying in a boat. Drifting, drifting, I watched the high sunlit windows or the firelight that flickered and glowed on the ceiling when the ward was falling asleep. Outside the hospital a late spring was invading the home-service world. Trees were misty green and sometimes I could hear a blackbird singing. Even the screech and rumble of electric trams was a friendly sound; trams meant safety; the troops in the trenches thought about trams with affection. With an exquisite sense of languor and release I lifted my hand to touch the narcissi by my bed. They were symbols of an immaculate spirit—creatures whose faces knew nothing of War's demented language.

For a week, perhaps, I could dream that for me the War was over, because I'd got a neat hole through me and the nurse with her spongings forbade me to have a bath. But I soon emerged from my mental immunity; I began to think; and my thoughts warned me that my second time out in France had altered my outlook (if such a confused condition of mind can be called an outlook). I began to feel that it was my privilege to be bitter about my war experiences; and my attitude toward civilians implied that they couldn't understand and that it was no earthly use trying to explain things to them. Visitors were, of course, benevolent and respectful; my wound was adequate evidence that I'd "been in the thick of it," and I allowed myself to hint at heroism and its attendant horrors. But as might have been expected my behaviour varied with my various visitors; or rather it would have done so had my visitors been more various. My inconsistencies might become tedious if tabulated collectively, so I will confine myself to the following imaginary instances.

Some Senior Officer under whom I'd served: Modest, politely subordinate, strongly imbued with the "spirit of the Regiment" and quite ready to go out again. "Awfully nice of you to come and see me, sir." Feeling that I ought to jump out of bed and salute, and that it would be appropriate and pleasant to introduce him to "some of my people" (preferably of impeccable social status). Willingness to discuss active service technicalities and revive memories of shared front-line experience.

Middle-aged or elderly Male Civilian: Tendency (in response to sympathetic gratitude for services rendered to King and Country) to assume haggard facial aspect of one who had "been through hell." Inclination to wish that my wound was a bit worse then it actually was, and have nurses hovering round with discreet reminders that my strength mustn't be overtaxed. Inability to reveal anything crudely horrifying to civilian sensibilities. "Oh yes, I'll be out there again by the autumn." (Grimly wan reply to suggestions that I was now honourably qualified for a home-service job.) Secret antagonism to all uncomplimentary references to the German Army.

Charming Sister of Brother Officer: Jocular, talkative, debonair, and diffidently heroic. Wishful to be wearing all possible medal-ribbons on pyjama jacket. Able to furnish a bright account of her brother (if still at the front) and suppressing all unpalatable facts about the War. "Jolly decent of you to blow in and see me."

Hunting Friend (a few years above Military Service Age): Deprecatory about sufferings endured at the front. Tersely desirous of hearing all about last season's sport. "By Jingo, that must have been a nailing good gallop!" Jokes about the Germans, as if throwing bombs at them was a tolerable substitute for fox-hunting. A good deal of guffawing (mitigated by remembrance that I'd got a bullet hole through my lung). Optimistic anticipations of next season's Opening Meet and an early termination of hostilities on all fronts.

Nevertheless my supposed reactions to any of these hypothetical visitors could only be temporary. When alone with my fellow patients I was mainly disposed toward self-pitying estrangement from everyone except the troops in the Front Line. (Casualties didn't count as tragic unless dead or badly maimed.) . . . I couldn't be free from the War; even this hospital ward was full of it, and every day the oppression increased. Outwardly it was a pleasant place to be lazy in. Morning sunshine slanted through the tall windows, brightening the grey-green walls. . . . Some officers lay humped in bed, smoking and reading newspapers; others loafed about in dressing-gowns, going to and from the washing room where they scraped the bristles from their contended faces. A raucous gramophone continually ground out popular tunes. In the morning it was rag-time—*Everybody's Doing It* and *At the Fox-Trot Ball*. (*Somewhere a Voice is calling, God send you back to me*, and such-like sentimental songs were reserved for the evening hours.) Before midday no one had enough energy to begin talking war shop, but after that I could always hear scraps of conversation. . . . My eyes were reading one of Lamb's Essays, but my mind was continually distracted by such phrases as "Barrage lifted at the first objective," "shelled us with heavy stuff," "couldn't raise enough decent N.C.O.s," "first wave got held up by machine-guns," and "bombed them out of a sap."

Although I have stated that after my first few days in hospital I "began to think," I cannot claim that my thoughts were clear or consistent. I did, however, become definitely critical and inquiring about the War. While feeling that my infantry experience justified this, it did not occur to me that I was by no means fully informed on the subject. . . .

It was May 2nd and warm weather; no one appeared to be annoyed about the War, so why should I worry? Sitting on the top of a bus, I glanced at the editorial paragraphs of the *Unconservative Weekly*. The omniscience of this ably written journal had become the basis of my provocative views on world affairs.

Nutwood Manor was everything that a wounded officer could wish for. From the first I was conscious of a kindly welcome. It was the most perfect house I'd ever stayed in. Also, to put the matter plainly, it was the first time I'd ever stayed with an Earl. "Gosh! This is a slice of luck," I thought. A reassuring man-servant conducted me upstairs. My room was called "The Clematis Room"; I noticed the name on the door. Leaning my elbows on the window-sill, I gazed down at the yew hedges of a formal garden; woods and meadows lay beyond and below, glorious with green and luminous in evening light; far away stood the Sussex Downs, and it did my heart good to see them. Everything in the pretty room was an antithesis to ugliness and discomfort. Beside the bed there was a bowl of white lilac and a Bible. Opening it at random to try my luck, I put my finger on the following verse from the Psalms: "The words of his mouth were smoother than butter, but war was in his heart." Rather an odd coincidence, I thought, that the word "war" should turn up like that. . . .

. . .

Nothing could have been more tranquil and harmonious than my first evening at Nutwood Manor. Nevertheless I failed to fall asleep in the Clematis Room. Lying awake didn't matter much at first; there was plenty to ruminate about; the view across the Weald at sunset had revived my memories of "the good old days when I hunted with the Ringwell." I had escaped from the exasperating boredom of hospital life, and now for a few weeks I could forget about the War. . . . But the War insisted on being remembered, and by 3 a.m. it had become so peremptory that I could almost believe that some of my friends out in France must be waiting to go over the top. One by one, I thought of as many of them as I could remember. . . .

I'd overheard Lady Asterisk talking about spiritualism to one of the officers; evidently she was a strong believer in the "unseen world." Perhaps it was this which set me wondering whether, by concentrating my mind on, say, young Ormand (who was still with the Second Battalion) I might be able to receive some reciprocal communication. At three o'clock in the morning a sleepless mind can welcome improbabilities and renounce its daylight skepticism. Neither voice nor vision rewarded my expectancy.

But I was rewarded by an intense memory of men whose courage had shown me the power of the human spirit—that spirit which could withstand the utmost assault. Such men had inspired me to be at my best when things were very bad, and they outweighed all the failures.

Against the background of the War and its brutal stupidity those men had stood glorified by the thing which sought to destroy them. . . .

. . .

I awoke to a cloudless Sabbath morning. After breakfast Lady Asterisk led me into the garden and talked very kindly for a few minutes.

"I am sure you have had a very trying time at the front," she said, "but you must not allow yourself to be worried by unpleasant memories. We want our soldier-guests to forget the War while they are with us."

I replied, mumbling, that in such surroundings it wouldn't be easy to worry about anything. . . .

. . .

Lady Asterisk liked to have serious helpful little talks with her officers, and one evening she encouraged me to discuss my immediate horizon. We were alone in the library. She listened to me, her silver hair and handsome face bent slightly forward above a piece of fine embroidery. Outwardly emotionless, she symbolized the patrician privileges for whose preservation I had chucked bombs at Germans and carelessly offered myself as a target for a sniper. When I had blurted out my opinion that life was preferable to the Roll of Honour she put aside her reticence like a rich cloak. "But death is nothing," she said. "Life, after all, is only the beginning. And those who are killed in the War—they help us from up there. They are helping us to win." I couldn't answer that. . . .

. . .

On the day before I departed from Nutwood Manor I received another letter from Dottrell. It contained bad news about the Second Battalion. Viewed broadmindedly, the attack had been quite a commonplace fragment of the War. It had been a hopeless failure, and with a single exception all officers in action had become casualties. None of the bodies had been brought in. The First and Second Battalions had been quite near one another, and Dottrell had seen Or-

126

mand a day or two before the show. "He looked pretty depressed, though outwardly as jolly as ever." Dunning had been the first to leave our trench; had shouted "Cheerio" and been killed at once. Dottrell thanked me for the box of kippers. . . .

Lady Asterisk happened to be in the room when I opened the letter. With a sense of self-pitying indignation I blurted out my unpleasant information. Her tired eyes showed that the shock had brought the War close to her, but while I was adding a few details her face became self-defensively serene. "But they are safe and happy now," she said. I did not doubt her sincerity, and perhaps they were happy now. All the same, I was incapable of accepting the deaths of Ormand and Dunning and the others in that spirit. . . . Nevertheless I left Nutwood with gratitude for the kindness I had received there. I had now four weeks in which to formulate my plans for the future.

At daybreak on June 7th the British began the Battle of Messines by exploding nineteen full-sized mines. For me the day was made memorable by the fact that I lunched with the editor of the *Unconservative Weekly* at his club. By the time I entered that imposing edifice our troops had advanced more than two miles on a ten-mile front and a great many Germans had been blown sky-high. To-morrow this news would pervade clubland on a wave of optimism and elderly men would glow with satisfaction.

. . .

Markington was a sallow spectacled man with earnest uncompromising eyes and a stretched sort of mouth which looked as if it had ceased to find human follies funny. The panorama of public affairs had always offered him copious occasions for dissent; the Boer War had been bad enough, but this one had provided almost too much provocation for his embitterment. . . . He made me feel that the world was in an even worse condition than my simple mind had suspected. . . . He explained that if he were to print veracious accounts of infantry experience his paper would be suppressed as prejudicial to recruiting. . . . He listened with gloomy satisfaction to my rather vague remarks about incompetent Staff work. . . .

When I inquired whether any peace negotiations were being attempted, Markington said that England had been asked by the new Russian Government, in April, to state definitely her War Aims and to publish the secret treaties made between England and Russia early

in the War. We had refused to state our terms or publish the treaties. "How damned rotten of us!" I exclaimed. . . . Markington was bitter against the military caste in all countries. . . . He told me that . . . if once the common soldier became articulate the War couldn't last a month. . . .

. . .

I had, so to speak, received the call, and the editor of the *Unconservative Weekly* seemed the most likely man to put me on the shortest road to martyrdom. . . . I began abruptly. "I say, . . . I've made up my mind that I ought to do something about it. . . . I don't see why I shouldn't make some sort of statement—about how we ought to publish our War Aims and all that and the troops not knowing what they're fighting about. It might do quite a lot of good,

mightn't it?" . . . He said, "I suppose you've realized what the results of such an action would be, as regards yourself?" I replied that
I didn't care two damns what they did to me as long as I got the
thing off my chest. . . . His words caused me an uncomfortable feeling that perhaps I was only making a fool of myself; but this was soon
mitigated by a glowing sense of martyrdom. I saw myself "attired with
sudden brightness, like a man inspired," and while Markington continued his counsels of prudence my resolve strengthened toward its
ultimate obstinacy. After further reflection he said that the best man
for me to consult was Thornton Tyrrell. . . . "What sort of man is
he to meet?" I asked dubiously. . . . "You'll find him perfectly easy
to get on with. A talk with him ought to clarify your ideas."

Early in the afternoon I left the letter at Tyrrell's address in
Bloomsbury. He telegraphed that he could see me in the evening, and
punctually at the appointed hour I returned to the quiet square. My
memory is not equal to the effort of reconstructing my exact sensations, but it can safely be assumed that I felt excited, important, and
rather nervous. I was shown into an austere-looking room where
Tyrrell was sitting with a reading lamp at his elbow. My first impression was that he looked exactly like a philosopher. He was small,
clean-shaven, with longish grey hair brushed neatly above a fine forehead. He had a long upper lip, a powerful ironic mouth, and large
earnest eyes. I observed that the book which he had put aside was
called *The Conquest of Bread* by Kropotkin, and I wondered what
on earth it could be about. He put me at my ease by lighting a large
pipe, saying as he did so, "Well, I gather from Markington's letter
that you've been experiencing a change of heart about the War." He
asked for details of my career in the Army, and soon I was rambling
on in my naturally inconsequent style. Tyrrell said very little, his
object being to size me up. Having got my mind warmed up, I began
to give him a few of my notions about the larger aspects of the War.
But he interrupted my "and after what Markington told me the other
day, I must say" with, "Never mind about what Markington told you.
It amounts to this, doesn't it—that you ceased to believe what you are
told about the objects for which you supposed yourself to be fight-

ing?" I replied that it did boil down to something like that, and it seemed to me a bloody shame, the troops getting killed all the time while people at home humbugged themselves into believing that everyone in the trenches enjoyed it. Tyrrell poured me out a second cup of tea and suggested that I should write out a short personal statement based on my conviction that the War was being unnecessarily prolonged by the refusal of the Allies to publish their war aims. When I had done this we could discuss the next step to be taken.

In *Siegfried's Journey* Sassoon recalls: "*I had scribbled a couple of notes which read as follows. Badly-wounded soldier, feeling glad about being safely out of the war—a citizen of life again—thinks 'Thank God they had to amputate.' . . . The notes were soon afterward developed into* The One-Legged Man *. . . , with a strong sense of satisfaction that I was providing a thoroughly caddish antidote to the glorification of 'the supreme sacrifice' and suchlike prevalent phrases. These performances had the quality of satirical drawings. They were deliberately devised to disturb complacency.*"

THE ONE-LEGGED MAN

Propped on a stick he viewed the August weald;
Squat orchard trees and oasts with painted cowls;
A homely, tangled hedge, a corn-stalked field,
And sound of barking dogs and farmyard fowls.

And he'd come home again to find it more
Desirable than ever it was before.
How right it seemed that he should reach the span
Of comfortable years allowed to man!
Splendid to eat and sleep and choose a wife,
Safe with his wound, a citizen of life.
He hobbled blithely through the garden gate,
And thought: "Thank God they had to amputate!"

132

To be arriving at a shell-shock hospital in a state of unmilitant defiance of military authority was an experience peculiar enough to stimulate my speculations about the immediate future. In the train from Liverpool to Edinburgh I speculated continuously. The self-dramatizing element in my mind anticipated something sensational. After all, a mad-house would be only a few degrees less grim than a prison, and I was still inclined to regard myself in the role of a "ripe man of martyrdom." But the unhistrionic part of my mind remembered that the neurologist member of my medical board had mentioned someone called Rivers. "Rivers will look after you when you get there." I inferred, from the way he said it, that to be looked after by Rivers was a stroke of luck for me. Rivers was evidently some sort of great man; anyhow his name had obvious free associations with pleasant landscapes and unruffled estuaries.

Slateford War Hospital was about twenty minutes in a taxi from Edinburgh. In peace-time it had been a "hydro," and it was a gloomy cavernous place even on a fine July afternoon. But before I'd been inside it five minutes I was actually talking to Rivers, who was dressed

133

as an R.A.M.C. captain. There was never any doubt about my liking him. He made me feel safe at once, and seemed to know all about me. What he didn't know he soon found out.

ADMITTING SECOND LIEUTENANT SASSOON, Siegfried, to Craiglockhart War Hospital on July 23, 1917, Captain W. H. R. Rivers entered the details of his "case" thus:

"Patient joined ranks of the Sussex Yeomanry on Aug. 3rd, 1914. Three months later he had a bad smash when schooling a horse, and was laid up for several months. In May 1915 he received a commission in the Royal Welch Fusiliers. He was in France from Nov. 1915 until Aug. 1916, when he was sent home with trench fever. He had received the Military Cross in June 1916. He was on three months' sick leave and returned to France in Feb. 1917. On April 16th, 1917, he was wounded in the right shoulder and was in the surgical wards of the 4th London for four weeks and then at Lady Brassy's Convalescent Home for three weeks. He then understood that he was to be sent to Cambridge to instruct Cadets.

"From an early stage of his service in France, he had been horrified by the slaughter and had come to doubt whether the continuance of the War was justifiable. When on sick leave in 1916 he was in communication with Bertrand Russell and other pacifists. He had never previously approved of pacifism and does not think that he was influenced by this communication. During his second visit to France, his doubts about the justifiability of the War were accentuated; he became perhaps even more doubtful about the way in which the War was being conducted from a military point of view. When he became fit to return to duty, in July of this year, he felt that he was unable to do so, and that it was his duty to make some kind of protest. He drew up a statement which he himself regarded as an act of wilful defiance of military authority: (see Times, July 31st, 1917). In consequence of this statement he was ordered to attend a Medical Board at Chester about July 16th, but failed to attend. It was arranged that a second Board should be held at Liverpool on July 20th, which he attended, and he was recommended for admission to Craiglockhart War Hospital for special treatment for three months.

"The patient is a healthy-looking man of good physique. There are no physical signs of any disorder of the Nervous System. He discusses his recent actions and their motives in a perfectly intelligent and rational way, and there is no evidence of any excitement or depression. He recognises that his view of warfare is tinged by his feelings about the death of friends and of the men who were under his command in France. At the present time he lays special stress on the hopelessness of any decision in the War as it is now being conducted, but he left out any reference to this aspect of his opinions in the statement which he sent to his Commanding Officer and which was read in the House of Commons. His view differs from that of the ordinary pacifist in that he would no longer object to the continuance of the War if he saw any reasonable prospect of a rapid decision.

"He had an attack of double pneumonia when 11 years old, and again at 14. He was at Marlborough College, where he strained his heart at football. He was for four terms at Clare College, Cambridge, where he read first Law and then History, but did not care for either subject. He left Cambridge and spent the following years living in the country, devoting his time chiefly to hunting and cricket. He took no interest in Politics. From boyhood he has written verses at different times, and during his convalescence from his riding accident in 1914 he wrote a poem called 'The Old Huntsman' which has recently been published with other poems under that title.

W. H. R. Rivers"

I WOULD GIVE A LOT for a few gramophone records of my talks with Rivers. All that matters is my remembrance of the great and good man who gave me his friendship and guidance. I can visualize him, sitting at his table in the late summer twilight, with his spectacles pushed up on his forehead and his hands clasped in front of one knee; always communicating his integrity of mind; never revealing that he was weary as he must often have been after long days of exceptionally tiring work on those war neuroses which demanded such an exercise of sympathy and detachment combined. Remembering all that, and my egotistic unawareness of the possibility that I was often wasting his time and energy, I am consoled by the certainty that he did, on the whole, find me a refreshing companion. He liked me and he believed in me.

I came down from Slateford by an early afternoon tramcar and spent a couple of hours strolling contentedly about the city, which happened to be looking its best in the hazy sunshine of one of those mild October days which induce mellow meditations. After my monastical existence at the hospital I found Princes Street a very pleasant promenading place. The War did not seem to have deprived Edinburgh of any of its delightful dignity; and when I thought of Liverpool, where I wandered about with my worries in July, my preference for Edinburgh was beyond question. The town-dweller goes out into the country to be refreshed by the stillness, and whatever else he may find there in the way of wild flowers, woods, fields, far-off hills, and the nobly-clouded skies which had somehow escaped his notice while he walked to and fro with his eyes on the ground. Those who live on the land come into the city and—if they are sensible people with an aptitude for experiencing—see it as it really is. It always pleases me to watch simple country people loitering about the London pavements, staring at everything around them and being bumped into by persons pressed for time who are part of that incessant procession which is loosely referred to as "the hive of human activity." All this merely indicates that although I arrived in Edinburgh with a couple of hours to spare and had nothing definite to do except to have a hair-cut,

nevertheless I found no difficulty in filling up the time by gazing at show-windows, faces, and architectural vistas, while feeling that I was very lucky to be alive on that serenely sunlit afternoon.

Writing about it so long afterwards, one is liable to forget that while the War was going on nobody really knew when it would stop. For ordinary infantry officers like myself there was always what we called "a faint bloody hope that it may be over in six months from now." And at Slateford there was always a suppressed awareness which reminded me that I was "shortening the War" for myself every week that I remained there. . . .

While I continued to clean my clubs, some inward monitor became uncomfortably candid and remarked "This heroic gesture of yours—'making a separate peace'—is extremely convenient for you, isn't it?" . . .

Against this I argued that, having pledged myself to an uncompromising attitude, I ought to remain consistent to the abstract idea that the War was wrong. . . .

At this point in my cogitations there was a commotion of thudding feet along the passage past my door, and I heard a nurse saying, "Now, now, you mustn't get upset like this." The sound of someone sobbing like a child receded and became inaudible after the shutting of a door. That sort of thing happened fairly often at the hydro. Men who had "done their bit in France" crying like children. One took it for granted, of course; but how much longer could I stay there among so many haunted faces and "functional nervous disorders"? . . .

I felt in my pocket for a little talisman which I always carried about with me. It was a lump of fire-opal clasped on a fine gold chain. Someone whose friendship I valued highly had given it to me when I went to France and I used to call it "my pocket sunset."

I had derived consolation from its marvellous colours during the worst episodes of my war experiences. In its small way it had done its best to mitigate much squalor and despondency. My companions in dismal dug-outs had held it in their hands and admired it.

I could not see its fiery colours now, for the room was almost dark.

But it brought back the past in which I had made it an emblem of successful endurance, and set up a mood of reverie about the old Front Line. . . . It seems to amount to this, I ruminated, twirling my putter as I polished its neck—that I'm exiled from the troops. . . . And I visualized an endless column of marching soldiers, singing "Tipperary" on their way up from the back-areas; I saw them filing silently along ruined roads, and lugging their bad boots through mud until they came to some shell-hole and pillar-box line in a landscape where trees were stumps and skeletons and no Quartermaster on earth could be certain of getting the rations up. . . . The idea of going back there was indeed like death. . . .

I argued it out with myself in the twilight. And when the windows were dark and I could see the stars, I still sat there with my golf bag between my knees, alone with what now seemed an irrefutable assurance that going back to the War as soon as possible was my only chance of peace.

BANISHMENT

I am banished from the patient men who fight.
They smote my heart to pity, built my pride.
Shoulder to aching shoulder, side by side,
They trudged away from life's broad wealds of light.
Their wrongs were mine; and ever in my sight
They went arrayed in honour. But they died—
Not one by one: and mutinous I cried
To those who sent them out into the night.

138

The darkness tells how vainly I have striven
To free them from the pit where they must dwell
In outcast gloom convulsed and jagged and riven
By grappling guns. Love drove me to rebel.
Love drives me back to grope with them through hell;
And in their tortured eyes I stand forgiven.

It would be an exaggeration if I were to describe Slateford as a depressing place by daylight. The doctors did everything possible to counteract gloom, and the wrecked faces were outnumbered by those who were emerging from their nervous disorders. . . . But by night they lost control and the hospital became sepulchral and oppressive with saturations of war experience. . . . One became conscious that the place was full of men whose slumbers were morbid and ter-

rifying—men muttering uneasily or suddenly crying out in their sleep. . . .

Shell shock. How many a brief bombardment had its long-delayed after-effect in the minds of these survivors, many of whom had looked at their companions and laughed while inferno did its best to destroy them. Not then was their evil hour; but now; now, in the sweating suffocation of nightmare, in paralysis of limbs, in the stammering of dislocated speech. Worst of all, in the disintegration of those qualities through which they had been so gallant and selfless and uncomplaining—this, in the finer types of men, was the unspeakable tragedy of shell-shock; it was in this that their humanity had been outraged by those explosives which were sanctioned and glorified by the Churches; it was thus that their self-sacrifice was mocked and maltreated—they, who in the name of righteousness had been sent out to maim and slaughter their fellow-men. In the name of civilization these soldiers had been martyred, and it remained for civilization to prove that their martyrdom wasn't a dirty swindle.

SICK LEAVE

When I'm asleep, dreaming and lulled and warm—
They come, the homeless ones, the noiseless dead.
While the dim charging breakers of the storm
Bellow and drone and rumble overhead,
Out of the gloom they gather about my bed.
    They whisper to my heart; their thoughts are mine.
    "Why are you here with all your watches ended?
    From Ypres to Frise we sought you in the Line."
In bitter safety I awake, unfriended;
And while the dawn begins with slashing rain
I think of the Battalion in the mud.
"When are you going out to them again?
Are they not still your brothers through our blood?"

When the moment arrived for me to take a deep breath and step discreetly in, I found Rivers looking as solemn as a judge, sitting at a table where he'd been telling the other two as much of my case

141

as he deemed good for them. In a manner which was, I hoped, a nice blend of deference and self-assurance, I replied to a few perfunctory questions about my health. There was a fearsome moment when the commandant picked up my "dossier"; but Rivers diverted his attention with some remark or other and he put the papers down again. The commandant looked rather as if he wanted his tea. I was then duly passed for general service abroad—an event which seldom happened from Slateford. But that was not all. Without knowing it, two-thirds of the medical board had restored me to my former status. I was now "an officer and a gentleman," again.

By the time I had been in Limerick a week I knew that I had found something closely resembling peace of mind. My body stood about for hours on parade, watching young soldiers drill and do physi-

cal training, and this made it easy to spend my spare time refusing to think. I felt extraordinarily healthy, and I was seldom alone. There had been no difficulty in reverting to what the people who thought they knew me would have called my "natural self." I merely allowed myself to become what they expected me to be. As someone good-naturedly remarked, I had "given up lecturing on the prevention of war-weariness"—(which meant, I suppose, that the only way to prevent it was to stop the War). The "New Barracks," which had been new for a good many years, were much more cheerful than the huts at Clitherland, and somehow made me feel less like a temporary soldier. Looking at the lit windows of the barrack square on my first evening in Ireland, I felt profoundly thankful that I wasn't at Slateford. And

the curfew-tolling bells of Limerick Cathedral sounded much better than the factory hooters around Clitherland Camp. I had been talking to four officers who had been with me in the First Battalion in 1916, and we had been reviving memories of what had become the more or less good old days at Mametz. Two of them had been wounded in the Ypres battle three months before, and their experiences had apparently made Mametz Wood seem comparatively pleasant, and the "unimaginable touch of time" had completed the mellowing process.

Toward the end of my second week the frost and snow changed to soft and rainy weather. One afternoon I walked out to Adare and saw for the first time the Ireland which I had imagined before I went there. Quite unexpectedly I came in sight of a wide shallow river, washing and hastening past the ivied stones of a ruined castle among some ancient trees. The evening light touched it all into romance, and I indulged in ruminations appropriate to the scene. But this was not enough, and I soon began to make enquiries about the meets of the Limerick Hounds.

At the end of the third week in January my future as an Irish hunting man was conclusively foreshortened. My name came through on a list of officers ordered to Egypt. After thinking it over, I decided, with characteristic imbecility, that I would much rather go to France.

144

I had got it fixed in my mind that I was going to France, and to be informed that I was going to Egypt instead seemed an anticlimax. I talked big to myself about Palestine being only a side-show; but I also felt that I should put up a better performance with a battalion where I was already known. So I wired to the C.O. of our second battalion asking him to try and get me posted to them; but my telegram had no result, and I heard afterwards that the C.O. had broken his leg the day after it arrived, riding along a frost-slippery street in Ypres.

Wednesday, February 13th. Left Southampton on Monday evening and got to Cherbourg by 2 a.m. Stayed last night at Rest Camp about three miles out, close to large château, used as Red Cross hospital. It is a mild grey morning with thrushes singing like spring. I am a little way from the camp, sitting on a bundle of brushwood under a hedge. The country round, with its woods of pine, oak, and beech, and its thorn and hazel hedges, might be anywhere in the home counties—Surrey for preference.

. . .

This is the third time in three years that I've been in France on February 13th. A magpie is scolding among the beeches, and the wind (south-west) bustles among the bare twigs. I have just recaptured that rather pleasant feeling of detachment from all worldly business which comes when one is "back at the War." Nothing much to worry and distract one except the usual boredoms and irritations of "being mucked about" by the army.

To-day we start our 1446-mile train journey to Taranto. It takes more than a week. My companions are Hooper, Howell and Marshall. Camp-commandant (promoted from sergeant-major to major?) asked us: "Anythink else you officers may wish to partake of? . . ." Have just picked a primrose. Wonder when I shall see another.

February 14. 6.30 p.m. Have been twenty-seven hours in the train. Not much room to move in our compartment, what with kit and boxes for provisions, which we use as tables and put our candles on. Marshall, very good at finding out things beforehand, bought

145

primus stoves, café-au-lait, and all sorts of useful things at Cherbourg. M. is the best of the three. About 21: big and capable; pockets usually bulging; hopes to be a doctor. Sort of chap who never grumbles—always willing to be helpful. I read most of the time, and they play cards continuously. . . . "Twist; stick," etc. . . . Halt at Bourges to draw rations. Have been reading Pater on Leonardo da Vinci! Funny mixture of crude reality and inward experience. Feel much more free to study other people than last time I was doing this sort of thing. More detached and selfless, somehow. But perhaps it's only because I don't play "Nap" and have been reading Pater—"this sense of the splendour of our experience and its awful brevity."

February 15th. Awake to find a bright frosty morning and the train in a station for an hour's halt. Crawled on to St. Germain (15 kilos from Lyons). Got there at 12.30 after going through fine country, fir-wooded hills and charming little valleys threaded by shallow rivers. Saw some oxen hauling a tree and a boy standing looking down at the train. The sun shone gloriously and warmed my face as I craned from the window to take in as much of this new part of France as I could. We stay at a rest camp near the station. Bath and lunch and then I went marketing with Marshall. The blue Saône or Rhône—don't know which it is—flowing nobly along. We leave again tonight. Am writing this in Y.M.C.A. hut after dinner. Entertainment going on. Jock sergeant reciting poem by R. W. Service; nervous lance-corporal sang "The truth or a lie, which shall it be?" in a weak voice without any emphasis.

DURING THE WAR as many as 600,000 British troops were stationed in Mesopotamia, and 500,000 of them ultimately were assigned to Palestine. Despite finally recovering Jerusalem from the Turks, their functions were less aggressive than defensive and colonial. Their job was to safeguard the Suez Canal from Turkish menaces and to keep one eye on the oil deposits of the Persian Gulf, access to which Britain required.

One of the most exciting things going on in this "warm-climate sideshow" was the performance of T. E. Lawrence—considered insane by most people in the Army—in stirring up the local Arab tribes to harass the Turks. But for most soldiers assignment to the Middle East—Gallipoli aside—was close to guard duty.

FEBRUARY 28. Arrived Alexandria after exactly three days' voyage.

A clear, gentle-coloured afternoon; blue sea; creamy, brick-red, terra-cotta, and grey city; wharves and docks with drifting smoke and thickets of masts and funnels. Sunshine, not glaring. Everything breezy, cheerful, and busy.

British officers watch it all for a while, nonchalantly—then go below for tea. I also; no more excited than the rest of them. . . .

Shall I find anything tremendous and heroic out here, I wonder? Troops in a warm-climate sideshow. Urbane, compared with France. Rather the same sort of thing as this dock with its glassy dark water and mild night air; stars, gold moon, dark ships, quiet lights, and sound of soldiers singing—safe in port once more.

March 28. Late afternoon. Quiet and warm. Frogs croaking in the wet ground up the wadi. Small thorn trees make clumps of young green up the terraces. At the end of the wadi there is a water spring; small rills sing their way down among the stones and over slabs of rock. Pippits and wheatears flit and chirp among the bushes, perch on rocks, or are busy in the olive branches. On my way home from a walk, a gazelle got up and fled uphill among the boulders; stood quite still about 500 yards away, watching me. Then trotted quietly away. A free creature.

.   .   .

Thus I describe my sense of peace and freedom. And as I finish writing, someone comes excitedly into the tent with the latest news from France.

The bulletins are getting steadily worse. Names which mean nothing to the others make me aware that the Germans have recaptured all the ground gained in the Somme battles.

April 10. Up at 3.30. Started 5.30. Reached camping ground at Ludd about noon. Clear dawn with larks singing; large morning star and thin slice of moon above dim blue hills. Firefly lights of camp below.

Starting off like that in the grey-green morning is delicious. One feels so fresh, with one's long shadow swaying on, and for the first two hours the country is green and pleasant. After Ramleh (a white town with olives and fruit trees and full of British) it was very hot and the road terribly dusty. No shadow at all now and one ached all over and felt footsore—marching between cactus-hedges with motors passing all the time and clouds of dust. At lunch the C.O. told a story about some friend of his who was in charge of a camp of Turkish prisoners; they gave trouble, so he turned a machine-gun on them and killed a lot. This was received with sycophantic ha-ha's from the captains. Queer man, his lordship.

Note. Sensations of a private on the march. Left, left; left-right, left. 110 paces to the minute. Monotonous rhythm of marching beats in his brain. The column moves heavily on; dust hangs over it; dust and the glaring discomfort of the sky. Going up a hill the round steel helmets sway from side to side with the lurch of heavily-laden shoulders. Vans and lorries drone and grind and blunder along the road; cactus-hedges are caked with dust. The column passes some Turkish prisoners in dingy dark uniform and red fez, guarded by Highlanders. "Make the ———'s work, Jock!" someone shouts from the ranks. . . . Through the sweat-soaked exhaustion that weighs him down, he sees and hears these things; his shoulders are a dull ache; his feet burn hot and clumsy with fatigue; his eyes are tormented by the white glare of the airless road. Men in front, men behind; no escape. "Fall out on the right of the road." . . . He collapses into a dry ditch until the whistle blows again.

April 23. Lying in my little bivouac . . . I watch dim shapes going along the dusty white road in blue dusk and clouded moonlight. As they pass I overhear scraps of their talk. Many of them thick-voiced and full of drink. Others flit past silently. Confused shouts and laughter from the men's tents behind; from the road the sound of tramping boots. The pallor of the sand makes the sky look blue. A few stars are visible, framed in the triangle of my door, with field-glasses and haversack slung against the pole on the middle. Sometimes a horse goes by, or a rumbling lorry. So I puff my pipe and watch the world, ruminating on what exists within the narrow bivouac of my philosophy, lit by the single lantern-candle of my belief in things like *War and Peace* and *The Woodlanders*.

Since last year I seem to be getting outside of things a bit better. Recognizing the futility of war as much as ever, I dimly realize the human weakness which makes it possible. For I spend my time with people who are, most of them, too indolent-minded to think for themselves. Selfishly, I long for escape from the burden that is so much more difficult than it was two or three years ago. But the patience and simple decency which I find in the ordinary soldier, these make it possible to go on somehow. I feel sorry for them—that's what it is.

For in our Division considerably more than half the N.C.O.s and

men have been on active service without leave since September 1915, when they went to Gallipoli. And now, as a nice change of air, they are being shipped back to the Western Front to help check the new German offensive. Obviously they have sound reasons for feeling a bit fed-up.

"Of course they have! That is why we are so grateful to them and so proud of them" reply the people at home. What *else* do they get, besides this vague gratitude? Company football matches, beer in the canteens, and one mail in three weeks.

I felt all this very strongly . . . when a Concert Party gave an entertainment to the troops. It wasn't much; a canvas awning; . . . two blue-chinned actors in soft felt hats—one of them jangling rag-time tunes on a worn-out upright; three women in short silk skirts singing the old, old, soppy popular songs; and all . . . of them doing their best with their little repertoire.

They were unconscious, it seemed to me, of the intense impact of their audience—that dim-brown . . . mass of men. Row beyond row, I watched those soldiers, listening so quietly, chins propped on hands, to the songs which epitomized their "Blighty hunger," their longing for the gaiety and sentiment of life. . . .

It was as though these civilians were playing to an audience of the dead and the living—men and ghosts who had crowded in like moths to a lamp. One by one they had stolen back, till the crowd seemed limitlessly extended. And there . . . they listen to "Dixieland" and "It's a long, long trail," and "I hear you calling me." But it was the voice of life that "joined in the chorus, boys"; and very powerful and impressive it sounded.

May 1st. (*S.S. Malwa, P. & O.* 10,838 tons, after leaving Alexandria for Marseilles. Three Battalions on board; also Divisional General, four Brigadiers, and numerous staff-officers. 3000 "souls" altogether not counting the boat's crew. Raft accommodation for about 1000. Six other boats in the convoy, escorted by destroyers.)

Scraps of conversation float up from the saloon below the gallery where I am sitting. "I myself believe. . . . I think, myself. . . . My own opinion is. . . ."

The speaker continues to enunciate his opinion in a rather too well-bred voice. The War—always the War—and world politics, plus a few other matters of supreme importance, are being discussed, quite informally, by a small group of staff-officers. (I know it is unreasonable, but I am prejudiced against staff-officers—they are so damned well-dressed and superior!) After a while they drift away, and their superior talk is superseded by a jingle of knives, forks, and spoons; the stewards are preparing the long tables for our next meal.

S.S. Malwa (not a name that inspires confidence—I don't know why), cleaving the level water with a perturbed throbbing vibration, carries us steadily away from the unheeding warmth and mystery of Egypt. Leaving nothing behind us, we are bound for the heavily-rumoured grimness of the battles in France. The troops are herded on the lower decks. . . . Unlike the Staff, they have no smart uniforms, no bottles of hair-oil, and no confidential information with which to make their chatter important and intriguing. *John Bull* and ginger beer are their chief facilities for passing the time pleasantly. They do not complain that the champagne on board is inferior and the food

151

only moderate. In fact they make me feel that Dickens was right when he wrote so warm-heartedly about "the poor." They are only a part of the huge dun-coloured mass of victims which passes through the shambles of war into the gloom of death where even generals "automatically revert to the rank of private." But in the patience and simplicity of their outward showing they seem like one soul. They are the tradition of human suffering and endurance, stripped of all the silly self-glorifications and embellishments by which human society seeks to justify its conventions.

GRAVES RECALLS: "I heard again, at the end of May, from France. Siegfried quoted Duhamel: 'It was ordained that you should suffer without purpose and without hope, but I will not let all your sufferings be lost in the abyss.' Yet he wrote the next paragraph in his happy-warrior vein, saying that his men were the best he'd ever served with. He wished I could see them. Though I mightn't believe it, he was training them bloody well and couldn't imagine whence his flame-like ardour had come; but come it had. His military efficiency derived from the admirable pamphlets now being issued: so different from the stuff we used to get two years before. He said that when he read my letter he began to think: 'Damn Robert, damn everyone except my company, the smartest turn-out ever seen, and damn Wales, and damn leave, and damn being wounded, and damn everything except staying with my company until it has melted away. Limping and crawling among the shell-holes, or lying very still in the afternoon sunshine in dignified desecrated attitudes.' He asked me to remember this mood when I saw him (if I saw him) worn out and smashed up again, querulous and nerve-ridden. Or when I read something in the Casualty List and got a polite letter from Mr. Lousada, his solicitor. There had never been such a Battalion, he said, since 1916, but in six months it would have ceased to exist."

MAY 14. Sitting in the Company Mess on a fine breezy afternoon copying out and assimilating a lecture on Consolidation of Captured Trenches, which I shall spout to the Company as though it came out of my head, though it is all from the recently issued *Manual for the training and employment of Platoons* which I spent yesterday evening in studying. I now feel rather "on my toes" about being in France, and am resolved to make a good job of it this time. The manual (a 32-page pamphlet) is a masterpiece of common sense, clearness, and condensation, and entirely supersedes the academic old *Infantry Training 1914* which was based on Boer War experience and caused me much mystification. Having just evolved an alliterative axiom— "clear commands create complete control"—I sit at the window watching soldiers going up and down the lane; now and then a lorry passes, or a peasant with a grey horse. On the opposite side of the road is a fine hawthorn hedge and an orchard containing two brown cows munching lush grass. A little way off, the church bell begins tolling.

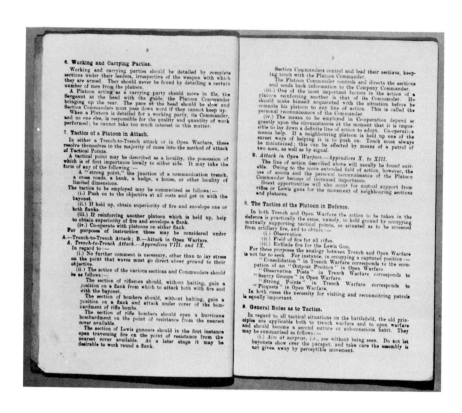

I tell myself that I simply must become an efficient company commander. It is the only way I can do the men any good, and they are such a decent well-behaved lot that it is a pleasure to work with them and do what one can for their comfort.

I look out at the falling rain and the grey evening beyond the churchyard wall and wonder if anything awaits me that will be more truly human than my sense of satisfaction yesterday at Rue railway station. What did I do to gain that feeling? . . . There were five of my men who had come too late to get any tea. Disconsolately they stood at the empty dixy—tired out by the long march and herded into a dirty van to be carried a bit nearer to hell. But I managed to get some hot tea for them. Alone I did it. Without me they would have got none. And for the moment the War seemed worth while! . . . That sort of thing reminds me of my servant and the numberless small worries and exasperations which he has saved me from in the past ten weeks. Nothing could be better than the way he does things, quiet and untiring. He is simple, humble, patient, and brave. He is reticent but humorous. How many of us can claim to possess these qualities and ask no reward but a smile? It might have been of him that Duhamel wrote—"he waged his own war with the divine patience of a man who had waged the great world-war, and who knows that victory will not come right away." His name is 355642 Pte. John Bond. I write it here in case I am killed.

Odd that I should find myself back here, only a mile or two away from where I was wounded (and the Front Line a mile or two farther back after 14 months' fighting!).

I have returned into the past, but none of my old friends are here. I am looking across to the ridge where Ormand and Dunning and all those others were killed. Nothing can bring them back; and I come blundering into it all again to guffaw with a Canadian captain. The old crowd are gone; but young "Stiffy" and Howitt are just as good.

Expect I'll see more than enough of this sector, so I won't de-

scribe it in detail. The landscape is the deadly conventional Armageddon type. Low green-grey ridges fringed with a few isolated trees, half-smashed; a broken wall here and there—straggling dull-grey silhouettes which were once French villages. Then there are open spaces broken only by ruined wire-tangles, old trenches, and the dismal remains of an occasional rest camp of huts.

THE INFLUENZA EPIDEMIC of 1918 which Sassoon mentions in passing actually killed more people worldwide than the war itself: some twenty million are said to have died, most of them in India. The disease spread across Europe, killing 150,000 in England, 1,700 of them in one day. Some said the scourge emanated from the lice- and rat-infested trenches in Flanders and Picardy, others that it started in a similar unclean place, the slums of Bombay. The casualty lists in the London newspapers now added civilian deaths from flu to the usual military figures, and in one army, the American, more soldiers were carried off by flu (62,000) than by battle (48,909).

I NEVER WENT BACK to those trenches in front of Neuville-Vitasse.

The influenza epidemic defied all operation orders of the Divisional staff, and during the latter part of June more than half the men in our brigade were too ill to leave their billets. Owing to the fact that I began a new notebook after June 14th, and subsequently lost it, no contemporary record of my sensations and ideas is available; so I must now write the remainder of this story out of my head.

The first episode which memory recovers from this undiaried period is a pleasant one. I acquired a second-in-command for my company.

Hitherto no such person had existed, and I was beginning to feel the strain. In that private life of mine which more or less emerges from my diary, solemn introspection was getting the better of my sense of humour.

But now a beneficent presence arrived in the shape of Velmore,

and I very soon began to say to myself that I really didn't know what I'd have done without him. It was like having an extra head and a duplicate pair of eyes. Velmore was a tall, dark young man who had been up at Oxford for an academic year when the outbreak of war interrupted his studies. More scholastic than soldier-like in appearance (mainly because he wore spectacles) he had the look of someone who might some day occupy a professorial chair. His previous experience at the front gave him a solid basis of usefulness, and to this was added a temperament in which kindliness, humour, and intelligence divided the honours equally, with gentleness and modesty in readiness to assert themselves by the power of non-assertion.

With these valuable qualities he combined—to my astonishment and delight—what in conventional military circles might have been described as "an almost rabid love of literature." To hear poetry talked about in our company mess was inded a new experience for me. But Velmore, on his very first evening, calmly produced Flecker's poems from his pocket and asked young "Stiffy" if he had ever read *The Golden Journey to Samarkand.* When he volunteered to read some of it aloud the junior officers exchanged embarrassed glances and took an early opportunity to leave me alone with my second-in-command, who was soon enunciating, with ingratiating gusto:

> Across the vast blue shadow-sweeping plain
> The gathered armies darken through the grain
> Swinging curved swords and dragon-sculptured spears,
> Footmen, and tiger-hearted cavaliers.

A paraphrase of the last two lines became Velmore's stock joke when reporting that the company was on parade and it was a great consolation to me to hear that fine body of men described as "the footmen with their dragon-sculptured spears." But Velmore was never anything else but a consolation to me.

With an all-pervading sense of relief I used to smoke my pipe and watch him doing the office-work for me. Whenever an automatic annoyance arrived from Orderly Room I merely passed it on and he squared it up with facetious efficiency.

VIVIAN DE SOLA PINTO, Sassoon's "Velmore," *first encountered the name of his future company commander in the summer of 1917 when he was convalescing from a wound in Dieppe:* "One day," *he remembers,* "I picked up a magazine. . . . Turning over the pages idly, I came across a poem by a writer with the resonant name of Siegfried Sassoon, of whom I had never heard before. It was an attractive piece of verse," *he says, quoting the very lines,*

> *Return to greet me, colours that were my joy,*
> *Not in the woeful crimson of men slain, etc.,*

which Graves had found unpersuasive. "It seemed to me," *Pinto concludes,* "that this was a poet who was to be watched."

A little later Pinto came across a review of Sassoon's book The Old Huntsman. *The review quoted "Blighters":*

> The House is crammed: tier beyond tier they grin
> And cackle at the Show, while prancing ranks
> Of harlots shrill the chorus, drunk with din:
> 'We're sure the Kaiser loves our dear old Tanks!'
>
> I'd like to see a Tank come down the stalls,
> Lurching to rag-time tunes, or 'Home, sweet Home,'
> And there'd be no more jokes in Music-halls
> To mock the riddled corpses round Bapaume.

Pinto found he liked this better than "Return to greet me." "Here was a man," he says, "who had found the supremely right words for the growing indignation of the men of the front line at the heartless vulgarity of the people at home who were enjoying 'a lovely war.' I cut the poem out . . . and learnt it by heart."

Some time later, arriving for duty at the headquarters of the Royal Welch Fusiliers, Pinto was told, "You're to go to 'A' Company as second-in-command to Captain Sassoon."

"I pricked up my ears at these words. Could it really be possible that I should have the incredible luck of serving under the author of The Old Huntsman?

"The rest of that day had for me an apocalyptic quality."

Pinto and Sassoon spent their first evening talking poetry "until midnight." Pinto says: "He expounded what to me at that time was a kind of new gospel: Poetry must grow out of the realities of the human condition. Plain, direct language must be used and all inversions and archaisms must be avoided. . . . Of the younger poets he declared that by far the most promising was a young officer called Wilfred Owen whom he had met in hospital at Edinburgh. . . . I asked him what he thought of Eliot and he quoted with great gusto the poem beginning

> The readers of the Boston Evening Transcript
> Sway in the wind like a field of ripe corn."

AT ABOUT ELEVEN O'CLOCK I went out myself with Howitt and a couple of N.C.O.s, but it was only in order to get them accustomed to being out there. Everything was very quiet while we crawled along the company front in the wet corn. The Germans had sent over a few admonitory 5.9's just after "stand-down"; at long intervals they fired their machine-guns just to show they were still there. The topography of our bit of no-man's-land was mainly agricultural, so our patrolling was easy work. On the right, B Company were demonstrating their offensive spirit by using up a fair amount of ammunition, but I had given orders that not a shot was to be fired by our Company. An impressively menacing silence prevailed, which, I hoped, would impress the Germans. I felt almost supercilious as I stood in the trench watching some B Company enthusiast experimenting with the Véry light pistol.

That was one of my untroubled moments, when I could believe that I'd got a firm grip on what I was doing and could be oblivious to the whys and wherefores of the war. I was standing beside Corporal Griffiths, who had his Lewis gun between his elbows on the dew-soaked parapet. His face . . . had the look of a man who was doing his simple duty without demanding explanations from the stars above him. Vigilant and serious, he stared straight ahead of him, and a fine picture of fortitude he made. He was only a stolid young farmer from Montgomeryshire; only; but such men, I think, were England, in those dreadful years of war.

After I'd been along to the sentry-posts a second time, I went
back to the headquarters rabbit-hole to find Velmore dozing, with
Flecker's poems fallen from his hand, and the sturdy little sergeant-
major dozing likewise in his own little rabbit-hole near by, while the
signaller brooded over the buzzer. Away from the shell-hole there was
another dug-out—larger, but not very deep—where we slept and had
our food. Everything seems to be going on quite well, I thought,
groping my way in, to sit there, tired and wakeful, and soaked and
muddy from my patrol, while one candle made unsteady brown shadows in the gloom, and young Howitt lay dead beat and asleep in an
ungainly attitude, with that queer half-sullen look on his face.

The thought of that candle haunts me now; I don't know why,
except that it seems to symbolize the weary end of a night at the War,
and that unforgettable remoteness from the ordinary existences which
we might have been leading; Howitt going to an office in the morning; and Velmore down from that idyllic pre-war Oxford with an
honours degree; and all those men in the company still unmobilized
from farms and factories and wherever else it was they had earned a
living.

I seem to be in that stuffy dug-out now, with Howitt snoring,
and my wakeful watch ticking on the wrist which supported my head,

161

and the deathly map of France and Flanders all around me in huge darkness receding to the distant boom of a big gun. I seem to be back in my mind as it then was—a mind whose haggard vigilance had the power to deny its body rest, while with the clairvoyance of sleeplessness it strove to be detached from clogging discomfort and to achieve, in its individual isolation, some sort of mastery over the experience which it shared with those dead and sleeping multitudes, of whom young Howitt was the visible representation.

I wanted to know—to understand—before it was too late, whether there was any meaning in this human tragedy which sprawled across France, while those who planned yet further slaughter were like puppets directing operations on which the unknown gods had turned their backs in boredom with our blundering bombardments. I wanted to know the reason why Corporal Griffiths was being what he was in quiet fortitude.

And I felt a great longing to be liberated from these few hundred yards of ant-like activity—to travel all the way along the Western Front—to learn through my eyes and with my heart the organism of this monstrous drama which my mind had not the power to envision as a whole. But my mind could see no further than the walls of that dug-out with its one wobbling candle which now burnt low.

Refreshed by a few hours' sleep, I was up in the Front Line an hour or two after midday, gazing at the incalculable country beyond the cornfield. My map told me that the town of Merville was about three miles away from me, but the level landscape prevented it from being visible. Our long-range gunners knew a lot about Merville, no doubt, but it was beyond my horizon, and I couldn't hear so much as a rumble of wheels coming from that direction. The outlook was sun-lit and completely silent, for it was the quietest time of day.

I was half-way between two sentry-posts, on the extreme left of our sector, where no-man's-land was narrowest. The longer I stared at the cornfield the more I wanted to know what was on the other side, and this inquisitiveness gradually developed into a determination. Discarding all my obligations as Company Commander (my main obligation being to remain inside the trench and get it deepened by those 120 shovels, which we'd taken over) I took off all my equipment, strolled along to the nearest sentry, borrowed his bayonet, and told him that I was going out to have a look at the wire. Returning to my equipment, I added my tunic and steel helmet to the heap, took a deep breath, grasped the bayonet firmly in my right hand, and crawled out into the unknown. I wasn't doing this from a sense of duty. It would certainly be helpful if I could find out exactly what things were like on the other side, and whether, as was rumoured by staff experts, the Germans withdrew most of their trench garrison during the day. But my uppermost idea was, I must admit, that the first man of the 74th Division to arrive in the enemy trenches was going to be me. This was a silly idea and I deserved no credit at all for it. Relying on Velmore to hold the fort at company headquarters, I was lapsing into my rather feckless 1916 self. It was, in fact, what I called "playing my natural game." I can't believe that I really enjoyed it, but it was exciting to worm one's way across. . . . After about 300 yards of this sort of thing I crept through a few strands of wire. . . .

The shallow German trench was only a few yards away, and there was no one in it, which was a great relief to my mind. I got into it as quickly as I could and then sat down, feeling by no means at home. The bayonet in my hand didn't seem to give me any extra confidence, but there were some stick-bombs lying about, so I picked one up, thinking that it would be just as well to take something back as a surprise for old Velmore. I then proceeded along the trench, sedately but bent double . . . The trench was only waist-deep; almost at once I saw what I presumed to be a machine-gun team. There were four of them, and they were standing about thirty yards away, gazing in the other direction. They were wearing flat blue-grey caps and their demeanour suggested boredom and idleness. Anyhow I was at last more or less in contact with the enemies of England. I had come from Edinburgh via Limerick and Jerusalem, drawing full pay for seven months, and I could now say that I had seen some of the people I was fighting against. And what I saw was four harmless young Germans who were staring up at a distant aeroplane.

Standing upright, I watched them with breathless interest until one of them turned and looked me straight in the face. He was a blond youth of Saxon type, and he registered complete astonishment. For several seconds we gaped at one another; then he turned to draw the attention of his companions to their unknown visitor, who immediately betook himself to the cover of the cornfield, to the best of his ability imitating a streak of light. I returned much quicker than I came, and while the Germans were talking it over at their leisure I resumed my tunic and tin hat and took the bayonet back to its owner who eyed the stick-bomb enquiringly. With a marked change of manner from my recent retreat on all fours, I laconically mentioned that I'd just slipped across and fetched it. I then returned in triumph to Velmore, who implored me not to do that sort of thing again without warning him.

We thereupon decided that, as the general had announced that he expected a prisoner as soon as possible, the obvious thing to do was to send Howitt across with a strong patrol some fine morning to bring back that machine-gun team and thus acquire a Military Cross. It had been great fun, I felt. And I regarded myself as having scored a point against the people who had asserted that I was suffering from shell-shock.

On the following night . . . we were agreeing that the company was getting through its first dose of the line extremely well. They were a fine steady lot, and had worked hard at strengthening the posts and deepening the shallow connecting trench. We had also improved the wire. Best of all, we should be relieved the next night. "And not a single casualty so far," said Velmore. I didn't touch wood, but as to-morrow was the thirteenth I produced my fire-opal and touched that. "Aren't opals supposed to be unlucky?" he enquired dubiously, shutting one eye while he admired the everlasting sunset glories of the jewel. "Mine isn't," I replied, adding that I intended to give it another test that night. "I'm going to do a really good patrol," I announced. Velmore looked worried and said he wished I wouldn't. He argued that there was no special reason for doing it. I reminded him that we must maintain our supremacy in no-man's-land. "Haven't you already shown your damned supremacy by going over and quelling the Fritzes with a look?" he protested. But I produced a plausible project. I was going to locate a machine-gun which had seemed to be firing from outside their trench with the intention of enfilading us, and anyhow it was all arranged, and I was going out with Corporal Davies at one o'clock, from No. 14 post (which was where our company front ended). Seeing that I was bent on going, Velmore became helpful, and the sergeant-major was told to send an urgent warning to B Company, as the objective I had in mind was on their front.

My real reason for seeking trouble like this was my need to escape from the worry and responsibility of being a Company Commander, plus annoyance with the idea of being blown to bits while sitting there watching Velmore inditing a nicely-worded situation report. I was tired and overstrained, and my old foolhardiness was taking control of me.

To be outside the trench with the possibility of bumping into an enemy patrol was at any rate an antidote to my suppressed weariness of the entire bloody business. I wanted to do something definite, and perhaps get free of the whole thing. It was the old story; I could only keep going by doing something spectacular.

So there was more bravado than bravery about it, and I should admire that vanished self of mine more if he had avoided taking needless risks. I blame him for doing his utmost to prevent my being here to write about him. But on the other hand I am grateful to him for giving me something to write about.

If my visual meditations included the face of Rivers I did not allow myself to consult him as to the advisability of avoiding needless risks. I knew that he would have dissuaded me from doing that patrol. And then, no doubt, I dozed off until Velmore came back to tell me that it was getting on for one o'clock and Corporal Davies all ready for me up at No. 14 post.

Corporal Davies was a trained scout, young, small, and active. We had worked out our little scheme, such as it was, and he now informed me in a cheerful whisper that the machine-gun which was our objective had been firing now and again from its usual position, which was half-right, about four hundred yards away. (The German trench was about six hundred yards from ours at that point.) In my pocket I had my little automatic pistol to provide moral support, and we took three or four Mills' bombs apiece. Our intention was to get as near as we could and then put the wind up the machine-gunners with our bombs.

A sunken farm-road ran out from No. 14 post; along this we proceeded with intense caution. About a hundred yards out we forsook the road and bore right-handed. It was a warm still night and the moon was very properly elsewhere, but the clear summer sky diminished the darkness and one could see quite a lot after a bit. Under such conditions every clod of earth was liable to look like the head of a recumbent enemy and the rustle of a fieldmouse in the corn could cause a certain trepidation—intrepid trepidation, of course.

Obviously it takes a longish time to crawl three or four hundred yards with infinite caution, but as nothing occurred to hinder our progress there is nothing narratable about it. I hadn't the time on me; crawling on my stomach might have smashed my watch-glass if it had been in my pocket, and its luminosity would have been out of place on my wrist. But what a relief it was, to be away from time and its petty tyrannies, even when one's heart was in one's mouth.

Behind us loomed the sentry-posts and the impressive sweep of the line, where poor old Velmore was peering anxiously out while he awaited our return. It really felt as though Corporal Davies and I had got the best of it out there. We were beyond all interference by Brigadiers.

Just when I least expected it the German machine-gun fired a few rounds, for no apparent reason except to allow us to locate it. We were, as far as I could judge, less than fifty yards from it and it seemed uncomfortably near. I looked at Davies, whose countenance was only too visible, for the sky was growing pale and we must have been out there well over two hours. Davies needed no prompting. He had already pulled out the pin of a bomb. So, to cut a long story short, we crawled a bit nearer, loosed off the lot, and retreated with the rapidity of a pair of scared badgers. I don't for a moment suppose that we hit anybody, but the deed was done, and when we were more than half-way home I dropped into the sunken road, and only the fact that I was out on a patrol prevented me from slapping my leg with a loud guffaw.

. . .

Now that it was all over I was exuberantly excited. It had been tremendous fun, and that was all there was to say about it. Davies agreed, and his fresh young face seemed to be asserting not only our supremacy over no-man's-land, but the supreme satisfaction of being alive on a perfect summer's morning after what might be called a strenuous military escapade. Taking off my tin hat I allowed my head to feel glad to be relieved of the weight of the War, and there, for several minutes, we sat leaning against the bank and recovering our breath.

It seemed hardly worth while to continue our return journey on all fours, as we were well hidden from the German trenches; the embankment of No. 14 Post was just visible above the corn stalks and my conscience reminded me that Velmore's anxiety ought to be put an end to at once. With my tin hat in my hand I stood up and turned for a moment to look back at the German line.

A second later I was down again, half stunned by a terrific blow on the head. It seemed to me that there was a very large hole in the right side of my skull. I felt, and believed, that I was as good as dead. Had this been so I should have been unconscious of anything, but that idea didn't strike me.

Ideas were a thing of the past now. While the blood poured from my head, I was intensely aware of everything around me—the clear sky and the ripening corn and the early glow of sunrise on the horrified face of the little red-haired corporal who knelt beside me. I saw it all as though for the last time, and my whole body and being were possessed by a dreadful sense of unhappiness. Body and spirit

were one, and both must perish. The world had been mine, and the fullness of life, and in a moment all had been changed and I was to lose it.

I had been young and exuberant, and now I was just a dying animal, on the verge of oblivion.

And then a queer thing happened. My sense of humour stirred in me, and—emerging from that limbo of desolate defeat—I thought "I suppose I ought to say something special—last words of a dying soldier." . . . And do you know that I take great pride in that thought because I consider that it showed a certain invincibility of mind; for I really did believe that I was booked for the Roll of Honour. I need hardly say that I wasn't; after a bit the corporal investigated my head and became optimistic, and I plucked up courage and dared to wonder whether, perhaps, I was in such a bad way after all. And the end of it was that I felt very much better and got myself back to No. 14 Post without any assistance from Davies, who carried my tin hat for me.

Velmore's face was a study in mingled concern and relief, but the face of Sergeant Wickham was catastrophic.

For Wickham was there, and it was he who had shot me.

The fact was that his offensive spirit had led him astray. He had heard the banging of our bombs and had been so much on his toes

that he'd forgotten to go and find out whether we had returned. Over-eager to accomplish something spectacular, he had waited and watched; and when he spotted someone approaching our trench had decided that the Germans were about to raid us. I was told afterwards that when he'd fired at me he rushed out shouting, "Surrender—you ———!" Which only shows what a gallant man he was—though everyone knew that already. It also showed that although he'd heard me lecturing to the company N.C.O.'s on my "Four C's—i.e. Confidence, Co-operation, Common sense, and Consolidation"—he had that morning been co-operating with nothing except his confident ambition to add a bar to his D.C.M. (which, I am glad to say, he ultimately did).

I suppose it was partly my fault. Both of us ought to have known better than to behave like that. The outcome was absurd, but logical. And to say that I was well out of it is an understatement of an extremely solemn fact.

. . .

Thus ended my last week at the War. And there, perhaps, my narrative also should end. For I seem to write these words of someone who never returned from France, someone whose effort to succeed in that final experience was finished when he lay down in the sunken road and wondered what he ought to say.

I state this quite seriously, though I am aware that it sounds somewhat nonsensical. But even now I wonder how it was that Wickham's bullet didn't go through my skull instead of only furrowing my scalp. For it had been a fixed idea of mine that something like that would happen. Amateur psychologists will say that I had a "death-wish," I suppose. But that seems to me to be much the same as wanting peace at any price, so we won't argue about it.

Anyhow I see a sort of intermediate version of myself, who afterwards developed into what I am now; I see him talking volubly to Velmore and Howitt on the way back to company H. Q.; and saying good-bye with a bandaged head and assuring them that he'd be back in a week or two, and then walking down to battalion H.Q., with his faithful batman Bond carrying his haversack and equipment; and then talking rather wildly to the Adjutant and Major Evans (who was now in command), and finally getting into the motor ambulance which took him to the casualty clearing station.

And two days later he is still talking rather wildly, but he is talking to himself now, and scribbling it down with a pencil as he lies in a bed at No. 8 Red Cross Hospital Boulogne.

And still the memory of the Company haunts me and wrings my heart and I hear them saying, "When's the Captain coming back?" It seems as if there's nothing to go back to in England as long as the War goes on. Up in the line I was at least doing something real, and I had lived myself into a feeling of responsibility—inefficient and impulsive though I was when in close contact with the Germans. All that was decent in me disliked leaving Velmore and Howitt and the troops. But now I begin to tell myself that perhaps half of them will be casualties by the time I get back, and I ask how many officers there are in the battalion who would refuse to go to England if it were made easy for them.

Not one, I believe; so why should I be the only one? They'd only think me a fool, if they knew I'd gone back on purpose to be with them.

170

Yet it is the supreme thing that is asked of me, and already I am shying at it. "We'll be sending you across to England in a few days," murmurs the nurse while she is dabbing my head. She says it quite naturally, as if it were the only possible thing that could happen. I close my eyes, and all I can see is the door into the garden at home and Aunt Evelyn coming in with her basket of flowers. In a final effort to quell those cravings for safety I try to see in the dark the far-off vision of the line, with flares going up and the whine and crash of shells scattered along the level dusk. Men flitting across the gloom; low voices challenging—"Halt; who are you?" Someone gasping by, carrying a bag of rations—"Jesus, ain't we there yet?"—then he blunders into a shell-hole and crouches there while bullets hiss overhead. I see the sentries in the forward posts, staring patiently into the night—sombre shapes against a flickering sky. Oh yes, I see it all, from A to Z!

On February 13th I had landed in France and again became part of the war machine which needed so much flesh and blood to keep it working. On July 20th the machine automatically returned me to London, and I was most carefully carried into a perfect hospital.

There, in a large ward whose windows overlooked Hyde Park, I lay and listened to the civilian rumour of London traffic which seemed to be specially subdued for the benefit of the patients. In this apotheosis (or nirvana) of physical comfort, I had no possible cause for complaint, and my only material adversity was the fact that while at Boulogne I had hung my opal talisman on the bedpost and some-one had succumbed to the temptation. But the opal, as I reminded myself, had done its work, and I tried to regard its disappearance as symbolical.

. . .

Outwardly I was being suavely compensated for whatever exactions the war machine had inflicted on me. I had nothing to do except lie there and wonder whether it was possible to be more comfortable, even though I'd got a half-healed hole in my head. But inwardly I was restless and overwrought. My war had stopped, but its after-effects were still with me. I couldn't sleep, so after a few days I was moved into a room where there was only one other bed, which was unoccupied. But in there my brain became busier than ever; the white-walled room seemed to imprison me, and my thoughts couldn't escape from themselves into that completed peace which was the only thing I wanted. I saw myself as one who had achieved nothing except an idiotic anti-climax, and my mind worked itself into a tantrum of self-disparagement. Why hadn't I stayed in France where I could at least escape from the War by being in it? Out there I had never despised my existence as I did now.

And then, unexpected and unannounced, Rivers came in and closed the door behind him. Quiet and alert, purposeful and unhesitating, he seemed to empty the room of everything that had needed exorcising.

My futile demons fled him—for his presence was a refutation of wrong-headedness. I knew then that I had been very lonely while I was at the War; I knew that I had a lot to learn, and that he was the only man who could help me.

172

Without a word he sat down by the bed; and his smile was benediction enough for all I'd been through. "Oh, Rivers, I've had such a funny time since I saw you last!" I exclaimed. And I understood that this was what I'd been waiting for.

He did not tell me that I had done my best to justify his belief in me. He merely made me feel that he took all that for granted, and now we must go on to something better still. And this was the beginning of the new life toward which he had shown me the way. . . .

It has been a long journey from that moment to this, when I write the last words of my book. And my last words shall be these—that it is only from the inmost silences of the heart that we know the world for what it is, and ourselves for what the world has made us.

PHOTOGRAPH CAPTIONS
AND SOURCES

Photographs are from the Imperial War Museum
unless otherwise credited.

36 Lucy Elizabeth Kemp-Welsh, recruiting poster, "Forward!", 1915.

38 Siegfried Sassoon.

39 From *Instructions for the Training of Platoons for Offensive Action,* 1917 (Eileen Tweedy). Item "(h)" is worth noting.

40 Officer Cadet School, Trowbridge. The white cap-bands designate officer candidates.

41 28th Battalion, Royal Fusiliers, Public Schools Brigade, on a practice march, Nov., 1915.

45 *S S Victoria* (photograph courtesy of the Manx Museum).

46 Fatigue party fetching revetting hurdles from a dump. They will carry them forward (perhaps a mile or so) through communication trenches and use them to shore up crumbling trench walls.

47 Working party with waterproof sheets and trench waders. Such waders were standard issue for wear in flooded trenches. As Wilfred Owen wrote his mother from the Somme in 1917: "The waders are of course indispensable. In 2½ miles of trench which I waded yesterday there was not one inch of dry ground. There is a mean depth of two feet of water."

48 Near Miraumont, on the Somme, May, 1917. The mud is so bad here that a wooden road has been provided for the troops to march on.

49 Sebourg Chateau, near Valenciennes. Note the two guard-boxes, installed when the King made his French headquarters here.

51 Irish Guards at respirator drill, Amiens-Albert Road, Sept., 1916.

52 Aisle, Amiens Cathedral (J.-L. Boutillier, Comité départemental du Tourisme de la Somme).

52 Group Headquarters Dugout, 4th Brigade Australian Field Artillery, near Hill 60, Ypres, August, 1917. Because films and plates were slow and flash-photography primitive, pictures of dugouts, tunnels, funk-holes, and similar underground havens are rare. This dugout has clearly been in use for some time and is comfortably accoutred. Note the easel picture of the loved one on the table.

55 From London *Times*, March 27, 1916. D[avid]. C. Thomas, listed under "Died of Wounds" (lower left corner), is "Dick Tiltwood" (Eileen Tweedy).

56 Destroyed crucifix at Brie, March, 1917.

60 Before the assault on Thiepval, early morning, Sept. 15, 1916. The rocket patterns are left by red, green, or white flares or Very lights, sent up by the front-line infantry to signal fire directions to the artillery behind.

62 Lancashire Fusiliers in a front-line trench facing Messines, Jan., 1917.

62 The town of Morlancourt in 1918.

63 The Basilica at Albert, June, 1917. "The damaged tower of the basilica" was visible for miles and famous as a landmark, not least because of the

myths and rumors associated with the damaged gilded statue of the Virgin and Child on its top. The war would end, one prophecy held, when the statue finally fell to the street, and both Germans and British tried to bring it down with artillery fire. This failing, the Germans started the rumor that the side shooting it down would lose the war. The British finally shot it down—together with the tower—in April, 1918, to prevent the Germans, now occupying Albert, from using the tower as an observation post. Having done this, the British proclaimed that the Germans, exercising their well-known contempt for religious monuments, had wantonly destroyed it.

64 Sir Muirhead Bone (1876-1953), *On the Somme Near Montauban, In the Horse Lines*, black chalk and wash.

65 A man of the Lancashire Fusiliers in a trench facing Messines, Jan., 1917. This trench is deeper than usual, and the fire-step here is not just a raised earth ledge but a wooden platform. This man is wearing one of the newly fashionable "wrist watches," popular as a "trench requisite." His waders suggest the reason why the fire-step is elevated. "The fire-step was the front-fighter's couch, bed-board, food-board, card-table, workman's bench, universal shelf, only raised surface on which to set a thing down, above water level. He stood upon it by night to watch the enemy. He sat upon it by day to watch him in a periscope."—David Jones, *In Parenthesis*. Pvt. David Jones served in "B" Company of the Royal Welch Fusiliers, a unit very often adjacent to Sassoon's company. The two did not know each other.

65 Shell craters near Passchendaele, Dec., 1917.

67 From *Drill and Field Training*, 1916 (Eileen Tweedy).

69 Bombardment of Fricourt, Somme, July 2, 1916.

70 Leave train in a London rail station. One oddity of this war was the requirement that the soldier carry his full equipment with him—haversack, water-bottle, rifle, and all—when going on or returning from leave.

72 Wire-cutters for trench use.

73 Soldiers bathing near St. Elou, June, 1917.

73 Map-reading in a communication trench near Ploegsteert Wood, June, 1917. The wall of the trench is supported by revetting hurdles. Wire-cutters on the ground at lower right. Mills bombs on the ground at left. Of sandbags, empty and full, David Jones says in *In Parenthesis*: "Empty sandbags were used for every conceivable purpose. They were the universal covering. They were utilized as a wrapping for food; for a protection to the working parts of a rifle, and cover for a bayonet against rust. The firm, smooth contour of a steel-helmet was often deprived of its tell-tale brightness, and of its significant shape, by means of a piece of stitched-on sack-cloth. The sandbag could be cut open and cast over the shoulders against the weather or tied round the legs against the mud or spread as a linen cloth on the fire-step for a meal, or used in an extremity as a towel or dish-cloth; could be bound firmly as an improvised bandage or sewn together as a shroud for the dead. There remained the official use: they

177

constituted, filled with earth, the walls, ceiling, and even the floor surface of half our world."

78   Barbed wire near Langnicourt, Sept., 1917. Screw pickets like these, which could be twisted into the ground silently at night, were much preferred to the early wooden stakes, which had to be noisily pounded in with mauls.

79   German prisoners captured at La Boiselle, Somme, July 3, 1916.

80   The assault on La Boiselle, Somme, July 1, 1916. Many of the troops are carrying their rifles on their shoulders, believing that the attack is going to be, as they've been assured, a walkover.

81   Support troops moving to the attack, near Ginchy, Sept., 1916. Note that one attacks wearing full equipment. The age of the soldier at the lower left is notable. The minimum age was theoretically seventeen, but boys of sixteen and even fifteen were to be found at the front.

83   Remains of a German trench, Ypres sector, July, 1917.

85   Mametz Wood, August, 1916, some weeks after Sassoon experienced it and thus much more damaged. Photographs of it before it was reduced to matchsticks by shellfire are understandably rare.

87   From London *Times*, March 1, 1916 (Eileen Tweedy).

88   German artilleryman killed in Bourlon Wood, Sept., 1918.

90   Sir William Reid-Dick (1879-1961), bronze statuette of Robert Graves
91   ("David Cromlech"). The head is said to have been modelled from life in the 1930s. (Courtesy of Leo Cooper).

94-95   Near Ploegsteert Wood, June, 1917.

97   Ward in the No. 2 General Hospital, Le Havre.

101   Central Station, Liverpool (Liverpool City Council Libraries).

103   Cathedral Square, Rouen (Bibliothèque Municipale de Rouen).

105   F. Mantania, drawing, *Good-bye, Old Man*, in *Sphere*, June 24, 1916.

106   Trench near Arras, Feb., 1917.

107   Foot inspection by medical officer, near Roclincourt, Jan., 1918. Trench foot is caused by tight boots, cold, damp, and lack of exercise. As it worsens it develops into gangrene. (The right foot of the man being examined is in a dangerous way.) This trench wall is held up by wire mesh, and the men are sitting on a duckboard-covered fire-step. The men are wearing the most advanced form of gas mask, the "box respirator."

109   7th Battalion, Royal Fusiliers, near Mesnil, May, 1918.

110   Moving up along the Amiens-Albert Road, Nov., 1916. When an infantry company was on the march well behind the lines, its field kitchens, stoves on wheels, cooked its meals as it went.

112   Roadside ammunition dump, near Albert, July 1, 1916. Piled here are not merely cases of ammunition to be expended but used brass shell casings which will be shipped back to England for refill and return.

112 A YMCA soup stall, Mailly Maillet, Oct., 1916. The man second from the left is wearing one of the sheepskin coats "issued to the troops in the line," as David Jones notes in *In Parenthesis*, "against the cold. They were afterwards abandoned in favour of dressed leather ones, which, though far less fascinating, were less an abode for lice."

113 The road leading to Guillemont, Sept., 1916. Says David Jones: "I think the day by day in the Waste Land, the sudden violences and long stillnesses, the sharp contours and unformed voids of that mysterious existence, profoundly affected the imaginations of those who suffered it. It was a place of enchantment. It is perhaps best described in Malory—that landscape spoke 'with a grimly voice.'"

114 Carrying party, near Boesinghe, Aug., 1917. Many observers were struck by the sheer theatricality of proceedings at and near the front, noticing in many moments of the war a curious continuity with the long and noble British stage tradition. Thus David Jones: "No one, I suppose, however much not given to association, could see infantry in tin-hats, with groundsheets over their shoulders . . . , and not recall

' . . . or may we cram,
Withing this wooden O . . .'"

115 German dead near Pilckem, July 31, 1917.

117 Regimental Aid Post near Albert, August, 1918.

118-119 Advanced Dressing Station near Arras, April, 1917. German prisoners are helping with the stretcher-bearing.

118-119 Battlefield at Thiepval, Sept., 1916.

121 J. Hodgson Lobley (1878-1954), *Outside Charing Cross Station*, July, 1916, oil on canvas. The newspaper placards at lower right are telling what a great success the Somme attack has been.

122 Ward in a hospital of the Royal Flying Corps.

127 From London *Times*, March 20, 1916 (Eileen Tweedy).

129 H. W. Massingham ("Markington"), editor of *The Nation* (Jonathan Cape Publishers, Ltd., and the Executors of the H. W. Massingham Estate).

131 Bertrand Russell ("Tyrrell") (George Allen and Unwin, Publishers, Ltd.).

132 Convalescent soldier at the 4th General Hospital.

133 Letter from Sassoon to Robert Ross, July 26, 1917.

134 Captain W. H. R. Rivers, Royal Army Medical Corps.

137 Princes Street, Edinburgh (Courtesy Edinburgh City Libraries).

139 Troops of the Notts and Derby Regiment, near Brie, March, 1917.

139 British dead outside a dugout, Somme area.

140 An Australian soldier, wounded and shell-shocked, at an advanced dressing station near Ypres, Sept., 1917.

142 Sir William Orpen (1878-1931), *A Man with a Cigarette*, black chalk, pencil, and water-colour.

143 Augustus John (1878-1961), *Walking Soldier with Pack*, black and white chalk on sanded paper (Agnes Etherington Art Centre, Queen's University at Kingston).

144 Adare Abbey, County Limerick (Photograph courtesy Bord Fáilte, Irish Tourist Board).

147 Alexandria Harbour from *S S Bornu*, July, 1915.

149 Turkish prisoners at a supply dump, Kantara, 1918.

150 Concert party performing at No. 14 Convalescent Hospital, Trouville, Aug., 1918.

152 Troops aboard *TSS Norman* returning from the Mediterranean, March, 1919.

154 From *Instructions for the Training of Platoons for Offensive Action, 1917* (Eileen Tweedy).

155 Sir William Orpen, *Soldier Resting: The Road to Arras*, charcoal.

157 Vivian de Sola Pinto ("Velmore"), on sick leave, Hampstead Heath, 1917. (Hutchinson and Co., Ltd., Publishers).

160 Lewis gunner in a trench on the Somme, near Ovillers, July, 1916.

161 Battlefield, Aisne, June, 1918.

162 British dead awaiting burial in a cemetery near Monchy-le-Preux, Aug. 29, 1918.

168-169 Battlefield at night, near Thiepval, Aug., 1916.

171 Glyn Philpot, portrait of Siegfried Sassoon, 1917 (Fitzwilliam Museum, Cambridge). As Sassoon writes in *Siegfried's Journey:* "At the end of a sitting [in July, 1917], Philpot—putting away his palette and brushes—unobtrusively informed me that the portrait was completed. Inspecting it for the first time (I had conscientiously avoided looking at it before), I remarked that it was rather Byronic. 'You are rather, aren't you?' he replied, gazing at me with dark, heavy-lidded eyes which seemed courteously observant rather than keenly scrutinizing. I assured him that I should very much like to be, adding that there was no need to tell him how good I thought the picture. While we were having tea I glanced at it occasionally with a pleasant feeling that I had acquired a romantic, illustrative personality to preside over my published works. It was indeed an ideal 'posterity portrait.' "

171 D. Gordon Shields, portrait of W. H. R. Rivers (The Master and Fellows, St. John's College, Cambridge).